The

Feminine

Occult

The Feminine Occult

A Collection of Women Writers on the Subjects of
Spirituality, Mysticism, Magic, Witchcraft, the Kabbalah,
Rosicrucian and Hermetic Philosophy, Alchemy, Theosophy,
Ancient Wisdom, Esoteric History and Related Lore

By
Helena P. Blavatsky, Annie Besant, Florence Farr, Margaret
Murray, Mabel Collins, Lady Archibald Campbell, Katherine
Hillard, Jessie Horne, Edith Wheeler, Mary L. Lewes, Louise
A. Off, Sarah F. Gordon, Lydia Bell and Mrs. J. Allsopp

Lamp of Trismegistus

ISBN: 978-1-63118-711-7

Table of Contents

Introduction

Presented here is a collection of essays on a variety of related subjects, for students of the Esoteric sciences.

The word "esoteric" can be difficult to define. Esotericism in general can be seen less as a system of beliefs and more as a category, which encompasses numerous, different systems of beliefs. It's a bit of juxtaposition, since the word "esoteric" indicates something that few people know about, while the term itself broadly covers numerous philosophies, practices, areas of study and belief systems.

In a greater sense, Esotericism acts as a storehouse for secret knowledge, which is often considered ancient (by *tradition, if not by fact),* passed down from generation to generation, in private. At various times in history, simply possessing the knowledge of some of these subjects, was considered illegal and a jailable offence, if discovered. This usually included such general topics as Alchemy, Qabalah, Hermeticism, Occultism, Ceremonial Magic, Astrology, Divination, Rosicrucianism and so on. Collectively, these areas of study were often referred to as the esoteric sciences.

Sometimes, the outer garment of a subject isn't esoteric, while what is hidden beneath it, is. As an example, Freemasonry isn't necessarily esoteric by nature (at *least not anymore),* but certain signs, passwords and handshakes given to the candidate during their initiation, are in fact, esoteric, in the sense that they are hidden from the general public.

Today, in the twenty-first century, such topics are readily available at bookstores across the country, and numerous main-steam publishers offer beginners guides and coffee-table volumes on many of these subjects, intended for mass appeal. Books like "The Secret" have turned previously arcane topics into household knowledge. All that being the case, however, it isn't to say that there still aren't buried secrets to uncover, ancient wisdom being ignored and forgotten mysteries to be explored. In fact, it is often that we are only able to further our own studies by standing on the shoulders of these disappearing giants.

Lamp of Trismegistus is doing its part to help preserve humanity's esoteric history by making some of these classics available to those students who are seeking to unearth the knowledge of these ancient colossi.

So, be sure to check out other titles from us in our Esoteric Classics series, as well as our Rosicrucian Collection, Theosophical Classics and our Foundations of Freemasonry Series.

Preface

Though often overlooked in the history of western esotericism, women made a strong showing during the nineteenth century occult revival. Notable women such as Madame Blavatsky and Annie Besant certainly stand out, even to this day, as vanguards. This collection is intended not only to showcase some of their writing but demonstrate that women's involvement in occult publishing isn't something new.

Frequently women writers are left out of the framework, when it comes to discussing modern occult history. But the reality is that they've nearly always been present; in fact, one could say their collective presence was prevalent throughout the mid-to-late nineteenth century and into the early twentieth, nearly a century or more before the Age of Aquarius and writers like Linda Goodman and Starhawk became household names. Long before new age metaphysics and modern wicca took ahold of bookstore shelves, there were more than a few women pioneers in the field of occult authorship. And, while a few names have risen to the top and strongly stood the test of time, others failed to cement a legacy for themselves and sadly faded into the background.

During the time period of much of these essays, it was a common practice amongst esoteric writers, men and women alike, to straddle the fence between fiction and nonfiction. Often times writers would publish a tale that was clearly fictitious, while including real, living persons of the time, and claim that it was a real tale told to them, proving real occult powers. Similarly, sometimes, an occult writer of this era took a lot more liberties than one would today, with the inclusion of flowery prose, in their nonfiction. A case in point would probably be the regular inclusion of personal ghost stories (*or other supernatural creatures, be it vampires, fairy folk or some ill-defined spirits*) being used as anecdotal evidence to prove the existence of the paranormal or of a specific individual's psychic or occult powers. Or, simply as a reinforcement that otherworldly events are always happening around us.

Another notable feature adopted by many of the occult writers from this time period is that the they often wrote about Christianity in a much more mystical and enlightened manner than we encounter today. While learned men and women of the West were slowly being exposed to Eastern religions for the first time, the esoteric writers of the day began reinterpreting Christianity in a much more open-minded and inclusive manner than previous generations had. They were examining the *spiritual* aspects of the religion they had all grown up with and began to abandon the *literal* aspects of the scriptures. They were starting to see a spiritual world in which Hinduism, Buddhism and Christianity didn't clash but instead complimented each other. These writers spent much more time looking for similarities than differences. This loosening-up of their ideas, allowed them to embrace Theosophy and Spiritualism without entirely turning their back on the positive aspects that Christianity brought to the table.

And without the popularity of Theosophy and the first woman on this list, it's possible that occultism might have seen its return to the underground as quickly as it experienced its resurgence.

Easily the most notable woman in this collection is Madame Helena Blavatsky, who was a Russian occultist, prolific writer and co-founder of the Theosophical Society in 1875. She authored dozens of books and hundreds of essays for numerous theosophical periodicals of her day. Her two primary works, the *Secret Doctrine* and *Isis Unveiled* were practically mandatory reading for occultists at the time and are both still readily available today. It wasn't uncommon to find her contemporaries repeatedly quoting these books, at great length. Even today, she is still studied and enjoyed by many seekers.

Annie Besant was very active in the Theosophical Society, a Co-Mason, a prolific writer with dozens of books to her credit, she also regularly lectured around the world and was an early vanguard of feminism, decades ahead of her time.

Florence Farr was an actress, writer, a first-wave feminist of the late nineteenth and early twentieth centuries, as well as an active member of the British occult community who regularly worked with her male counterparts in the fields of esoterica, being an initiate of the Hermetic Order of the Golden Dawn.

Farr wasn't the only active member of the Hermetic Order of the Golden Dawn in this collection. Writer Jessie Horne was also initiated into the Golden Dawn, at the Isis-Urania temple in London.

Margaret Murray was an Egyptologist, an archaeologist anthropologist, historian, folklorist and first-wave feminist. She wrote on a diverse range of subjects including witchcraft and mythology. Here we are presenting a short translation of hers, dealing with Egyptian magic and mythology.

Mabel Collins was a novelist and playwright, often dealing with mystical themes in her fiction. She was theosophist and penned articles for the magazines of her time on numerous related topics ranging from eastern spirituality to various occult

11

subjects. She was a practicing medium of her time, and a reported lover of Jack the Ripper!

Lady Archibald Campbell was a well-educated socialite involved in British theater, with a strong interest in the folklore and magic of the British Isles. She regularly published in the Occult Review.

Katherine Hillard was a writer, lecturer and prominent Theosophist of her time, regularly contributing to various periodicals.

While some of the other women included in this book sadly didn't leave behind a large enough footprint to easily research their lives, they are nevertheless part of a greater tapestry, helping to preserve this important chapter of occult history.

These essays are but a mere example of those left behind by numerous women of their time, who demonstrated an active interest and involvement in a broad range of esoteric interests.

Enjoy then, this collection of women writing on subjects of the occult.

What Is Occultism?

by Helena P. Blavatsky

I believe Occultism to be essentially a reincarnation of ancient paganism, a revivification of the Pythagorean philosophy; not the senseless ceremonies and spiritless forms of those ancient religions, but the Spirit of the Truth which animated those grand old systems which held the world spellbound in awe and reverence long after the spirit had departed, and nothing was left but the dead, decaying body.

Occultism asserts the eternal individuality of the soul, the imperishable force which is the cause and sustaining power of all organization, that death is only the casting off of a worn-out garment in order to procure a new and better one.

So death, so-called, can but the form deface,

The immortal soul flies out in empty space,

To seek her fortune in another place.

Occultism, in its efforts to penetrate the arcana of dynamic forces and primordial power, sees in all things a unity, an unbroken chain extending from the lowest organic form to the highest, and concludes that this unity is based upon a uniformly ascending scale of organic forms of being, the Jacob's ladder of spiritual organic experience, up which every soul must travel before it can again sing praises before the face of its Father. It perceives a duality in all things, a physical and spiritual nature, closely interwoven in each other's embrace, interdependent upon each other, and yet independent of each other. And as there is in spirit-life a central individuality, the soul, so there is in the physical, the atom, each eternal, unchangeable and self-existent. These centers, physical and spiritual, are surrounded by their own respective atmospheres, the inter-sphering of which results in aggregation and organization. This idea is not limited to terrestrial life, but is extended to worlds and systems of worlds.

Physical existence is subservient to the spiritual, and all physical improvement and progress are only the auxiliaries of spiritual progress, without which there could be no physical progress. Physical organic progress is effected through hereditary transmission; spiritual organic progress by transmigration.

Occultism has divided spiritual progress into three divisions—the elementary, which corresponds with the lower organizations; the astral, which relates to the human; and the celestial, which is divine. "Elementary spirits," whether they belong to "earth, water, air or fire," are spirits not yet human, but attracted to the human by certain congenialities. As many physical diseases are due to the presence of parasites, attracted or produced by uncleanness and other causes, so parasitic spirits are attracted by immorality or spiritual uncleanness, thereby inducing spiritual diseases and consequent physical ailments. They who live on the animal plane must attract spirits of that plane, who seek for borrowed embodiments where the most congeniality exists in the highest form.

Thus the ancient doctrine of obsession challenges recognition, and the exorcism of devils is as legitimate as the expelling of a tape-worm, or the curing of the itch. It was also believed that these spiritual beings sustained their spiritual existence by certain emanations from physical bodies, especially when newly slain; thus in sacrificial offerings the priests received the physical part, and the Gods the spiritual, they being content with a "sweet-smelling savor." It was further thought that wars were instigated by these demons, so that they might feast on the slain.

But vegetable food also held a place in spiritual estimation, for incense and fumigations were powerful instruments in the hands of the expert magician.

Above the elementary spheres were the seven planetary spheres, and as the elementary spheres were the means of progress for the lower animals, so were the planetary spheres the means of progress for spirits advanced from the elementary--for human spirits. The human spirit at death went to its associative star, till ready for a new incarnation, and its birth partook of the nature of the planet whence it came, and whose rays illumined the ascendant—the central idea of astrology. When the lessons of a planetary sphere were fully mastered, the spirit rose to the next sphere to proceed as before. The character of these spheres corresponded to the "seven ages of man." But not always did the spirit return to the astral spheres. Suicides; those from whom life had been suddenly taken before fully ripe; those whose affections were inordinately attached to earthly things, etc., were held to the earth till certain conditions were fulfilled, and some whose lives had fitted them for such disposal were remanded to the elementary spheres, to be incarnated as lower animals, corresponding to the nature of their lives. Such were the perturbed spirits who sometimes disturbed the peace of sensitive mortals in the days gone by—perhaps now.

Transcending the planetary spheres were the three divine spheres where the process of apotheosis took place, where the spirit progressed till it reached the fullness of the Godhead bodily. From these spheres were appointed the

Guardians of the inferior spheres, the Messengers of God, ministering spirits, sent to minister to them who shall receive the inheritance of salvation.

Such is a brief outline of spiritual Occult philosophy; it may seem to be inconsistent with the ideas of modern Spiritualism, yet even Spiritualism has not altogether lost sight of the seven spheres and other peculiarities of the ancient astro-spiritual faith; and as knowledge is acquired and experience gained, a better understanding of both ancient and modern mysticism will bring them nearer together and show a consistency and mutual agreement which has never been disturbed—only obscured—by human ignorance and presumption.

But Occultism has a physical aspect, which I cannot afford to pass by. Man is a fourfold being.

Four things of man there are: spirit, soul, ghost, flesh;

Four places these four keep and do possess.

The earth covers flesh, the ghost hovers o'er the grave,

Orcus hath the soul, the stars the spirit crave.

When the spirit leaves the body, and is properly prepared for the stellar spheres, these are retained in the mortal remains; and the shade, which is no part of the spirit or the true man or woman, may still counterfeit them, make revelations of the past, in fact reveal more of its sensual history, and prove sensual identity better than the spirit itself could do, seeing it knows only spiritual things. The sciomancy of the past bears the same relation to modern psychometry that ancient Magic does to modern Spiritualism. Thus in haunted houses, in graveyards and places where deeds of violence have occurred, sensitives see the drama reacted which transpired long ago, the spirit being no accessory thereto.

The spirit cannot even communicate unless through the interblending of physical and spiritual aura, and only by coming *en rapport* with physical things can it know anything of them; and thus mediums are as necessary on the other side as on this; through which mediums, Guardian Spirits, we may gain a nearer apprehension of spiritual truths, if we live for them.

The Mysteries

by Annie Besant

Many and diverse have been and are the religions of the past and the present, the religions living and dead. One great difference one perceives in looking back over the history of the older past and comparing it with the history of more modern days: in the ancient times one does not come across anything in history of the nature of persecution of faith by faith. You find that each religion has its own kingdom, its own area, over which it rules. You find that a nation has its own faith, and that that faith lives in amity with other faiths of neighboring nations, unless it chanced that the nations themselves were at war. You find in imperial Rome, for instance, that a great Pantheon was raised, in which the Gods of every nation within the Roman Empire found each his place and each his cult. There might sometimes be jealousies and envies, but there was no idea that one religion was to rule over every nation; but rather that each nation naturally had its own particular faith and that the people of the nation worshipped their national God.

You find, looking back to those days, that if there was any trouble with regard to religion, then the origin of the trouble was political rather than religious. To leave the religion of the nation was equivalent to treason to the State; and so now and again you may find a man attacked and banished because of a change of faith. But that was rather because he denied his fatherland than because there was any wrong in thinking along his own lines on a question of belief; and it, is very noticeable that, in some of the most ancient faiths, it was held that, so far as intellectual acceptance of doctrine was concerned, the intellect might have free play, and there was no limit to the area over which the thought might extend.

On the other hand, in comparatively modern days, you find that religious persecution plays a great part in the history of rival faiths. You find many a missionary effort, many attempts to convert other peoples to a religion which is not the religion of their ancestors, and one not unnaturally demands: "Why this difference in the matter of tolerance between the ancient world and the comparatively modern? Why has this idea arisen that all people should accept a particular presentment of truth, that they should not follow an ancestral faith, but rather embrace one which is brought to them from other lands?"

And it is not without significance that the tendency to persecute in relation to religion is historically contemporaneous with the disappearance of the Mysteries from Europe. It was in connection with their gradual disappearance that you find arising the specter of religious persecution, so that one is inclined to put the two phenomena side by side, and to ask whether there may not be a relation between the disappearance of the Mysteries and the appearance of persecution.

When we come to enquire as to the difference between the exoteric faith and the esoteric teaching, when we come to look into the faiths of the past and to study the Mysteries of the past, we find that the faiths were just as different in the older world as they are different in the modern; but we also find that in relation to every faith there were Mysteries established, to which the most learned of that faith belonged, and in which the teachers of that faith were trained. We find, as we study still further, that though the outer presentment of religious doctrines in the exoteric faith differed with the nation, with the temperament and the traditions of the people, the teaching which made the Knower, the teaching which educated the Mystic, the teaching which gave knowledge instead of belief and enabled a man with full certainty to declare: "I know the things of the super-physical worlds" — we find that that teaching was everywhere one and the same, and that while the various exoteric faiths might differ, the inner heart of them, as found in the Mysteries, was the same. Just as you might, if you wandered round some great cathedral, see the light pouring out from window after window, and through every window a different color; as you might say, looking at that light streaming out through the glass: "The light in the temple is red", and another might cry: "The light in the temple is blue", and another would declare: "Nay, but the light is yellow", while another would asseverate that the light was purple; so with the exoteric religions of the world, each has its own color, each has its own presentment, and those who only see the outer religion declare that the religions differ, and that the light of truth that comes through each is not one and the same.

But just as if you go within the cathedral, if you penetrate within the shrine, you see that one white light is there and that the difference of the color is in the windows and not in the light, so do you see, when you enter into the Temple of the Mysteries, that truth is one though it may be presented in different fashions, and that though the colors of the faiths are various as the hues of the rainbow, inside the Temple of the Mysteries the white Light of Truth is one and the same. And it is, I think, because of that knowledge — which, inasmuch as it is knowledge of facts, cannot vary, while the language in which the facts are told will vary according to the speaker — it is because in all the ancient religions there was ever at the heart of them the Mysteries, giving the unity of truth and the unity of knowledge, it was because of that, that persecution for religious belief did not stain the older world; for the teachers knew there was the one truth, although the peoples might differ in their understanding of that truth veiled in garments of dogma, of ceremony, of varied presentment.

So one begins to think, if we are again in modern days to persuade the living religions of the world that they should form a Brotherhood and not a battlefield of warring creeds, that we must find a common place where all the religions may find their origin, where all the religions may find their teachers. We must hope and labor and aspire that that ancient institution of the Mysteries may once more be restored for the lighting and the helping of the world, and we must endeavor so to study and so to live that pupils may be found who shall draw down the Teachers from on high by the passion of their aspiration, by the purity of their lives, by the depth of their knowledge, who may thus show themselves worthy to be taught again by Men made perfect, to draw among themselves as Teachers, Those who have knowledge more than the knowledge of men.

Let us think, then, what the Mysteries were in reality. Let us glance for a few moments at the phases through which they have passed, and let us ask whether in our modern days it be possible to find material out of which pupils can be found to be taught. Never in the higher worlds is there grudging in the giving of the truth; never from above comes the check which prevents the pouring out of knowledge over the world. It is here, here in our lower world, here in these minds of men resistant of truth which they find it difficult to grasp; it is in the challenging, constantly questioning mind of our modern days; it is here that lies the difficulty in the restoration of the Mysteries; it is here that the barriers have been built up which check the free flow of truth.

This is not to be regarded as though it were outside the great Plan of the King of Evolution. There is naught outside that Plan; and if sometimes we think that things go ill, it is because our eyes are short- sighted, because we are not able to see the whole, and we judge only by a portion that we see. For in the great evolution of mankind, which lasts through millennium after millennium of our mortal time, in which days are tens of thousands of years, and in which a million years are but as yesterday to those great Minds that see over the whole of evolution; in the working out of such a Plan, in a gradual development of one stage after another, there is no stage which may be missed, there is no stage that is evil; each has its place in the long evolution, and the Architect who drew the Plan knows well the building that He is intending to erect.

It was necessary for human growth, necessary for the higher evolution of men, that there should be a period during which this mind of ours should develop the questioning, challenging, rebellious spirit without which it would not have conquered the knowledge of this lower world. It was well enough in days long gone by that child-nations should look up to divine Instructors, and obediently study the lessons given to them by those divine Men. But it was also well that the growing youth should develop the powers of manhood; and he could not have done it, had he always been kept in the leading-strings of Those greater than himself. So the time came when the Teachers said to the boy: "Go out, my son, into the world and find out for yourself what is the truth; develop within yourself the mind which is one aspect of the divine Spirit, and conquer by your own unaided strength the knowledge which the world can unveil before you; yours it is to conquer the lower world, yours it is to discover the laws of nature, yours it is to find your way while the guide for the moment is hidden."

But just as the father who sends out his son into the world watches over him with tender love and is ever ready to help when advice is needed, so was it with the Fathers of the race, those Elder Brethren who had reached perfection before the younger had climbed the ladder of evolution. They have ever been watching, although out of sight, withdrawn from physical vision but ever near and ready to help, and They have guided the nations as much through the times when Their forms were hidden, as They guided them when dwelling in the City of the Golden Gates of Atlantis, or in the White City of Shambala at the origins of our Indian Arya heritage.

But the times are changed and with the changing times a changing method. It has been said, and rightly said, that evolution is not a ladder of ascent but rather a spiral that ever returns upon itself higher and higher as evolution climbs. So it is that the past becomes again the present, but the present on a higher level than the road that humanity in the past has trodden, and the times are approaching when the Mysteries shall again be restored to earth, for the pupils are preparing today, and when the pupil is ready, as the old saying runs, the Master appears.

Think, then, of the times when the Mysteries were established on our globe and realize what was their function and their work. The outer religion, the religion of law of command, the religion that said "Thou shalt", or "Thou shalt not", that is, the outer religion that guides a man to righteous conduct by an authority imposed upon him from without, by moral codes, by laws of conduct which the man obeys oft-times without understanding their reason, obeys because a great Prophet has said so, because a Scripture has been written giving the precept, because a Church has proclaimed commandments, because a Tradition has declared: "This is the way, walk ye in it" — such a line of instruction, such a moral code, such a system of laws, makes the good man; makes the man who is the worthy citizen of the State, the man who is the loving husband and father in the home, the man who is ever ready to work for his country, who is looked up to as one of character and of noble life. But that is not the highest. A wise man in days long gone by declared: "The law was our schoolmaster to bring us unto Christ". A time comes in human evolution, when the work of the outer law is over because the law of the Spirit is unfolding from within, when the man no longer walks by an outer compulsion but by an inner direction, when the God within speaks, instead of the God without; and it is the function of the Mysteries to unfold the God within and to change man into the man made perfect, the man in whom the hidden God shines forth with manifested glory.

So we may read with reference to the Schools of Pythagoras that there were many who learned the outer teachings, who learned the civil and the social virtues, and so became the patterns of virtue that were the glory of ancient Greece. But that was only the outer court of the Temple; that was on the worldly side of the threshold of the Mysteries. For we read that there were other Schools, secret and hidden, into which, those who had reached goodness might be admitted, and in which the good man was developed into the God. That was the object of the Mysteries: to take the good man who had conquered all ordinary temptations, who had grown to a point where the world no longer either deceived or attracted, who had been able to develop within himself those essential virtues which are the bases on which everything else is to be erected — to take that man, to let him step over the threshold into the Temple. There they instructed him how the God within might unfold his powers, and how his garments of matter might be constructed so as to be vehicles for the forces of God instead of hindrances to those forces, as they are in the mass of the people in the world.

And then the man was taught, first of all, that he must purify the garments of matter that he was wearing, not only from the ordinary sins of men, not only from the ordinary passions of human kind, but that he must purify garment after garment of subtler and subtler matter, and learn to distinguish himself from the garments that clothed him, and consciously and deliberately to live in the house of matter of which he was the tenant and not the prisoner. For most men live as prisoners in the house of flesh that they wear.

They know not that there is a key that can open the gates; they know not that the key is hidden within themselves and is not held by anyone without. They think that death is the holder of the key, and that only when death comes, with that key which unlocks the body, can the Spirit arise free and immortal and know himself divine.

But in the Mysteries they were taught that the body was not a prison-house but only a dwelling- place; that the key could open the doors and man could walk forth at his will. So first they were taught by deep and profound meditation to draw the life away from the outer garments, and for a time to fix it in the inner and subtler garments that the Spirit wears. They were taught to separate the coarser from the finer; they were taught to evolve the finer senses as nature has evolved the physical senses for us through endless ages of years; and they were taught that the real powers of sight and of hearing resided in the spiritual man and not in the bodies that he was wearing, that the bodies had to be shaped into organs for the spiritual powers, and that each body was a barrier until the Spirit had redeemed the matter and formed it for its own purposes and as an instrument for itself.

Those true Mysteries which still exist — those which are ruled by the great White Brotherhood, the only people who have the right to say: "Enter", or: "Thou art not yet ready to enter" — those true Mysteries have never been withdrawn from earth, but have ever existed in the hands of these Men made perfect, who introduced Their neophytes into the realities of the higher worlds, and taught them consciously and deliberately to become familiar with those worlds of subtler matter, as the scientist of our days is beginning to become familiar with the physical world in which we live.

And today in those true Mysteries, when the doorway of Initiation is thrown open before the prepared pupil who has been led up to that gateway, the pupil passes out of the physical body, and is initiated first in the astral body, and is tested as to his knowledge of how to deal with the powers of that world, how to use its influences for human service. When you read, as you sometimes do, of the tests of the Mysteries, the ordeals of the Mysteries, realize that those are tests of knowledge and of power, not of the physical endurance which you read of in "occult" stories, the passing through fire, through water, through all the elements here: those are but the first and early tests on the astral plane for the pupil; they are not the tests of the man who has to show that he can control the powers of nature, and that they own him as their ruler because he has gained the knowledge which alone is able to control. For in any world, go where you will, be it this mortal world of men or be it the highest world of Nirvana, there is but one thing that gives power, and that is Knowledge. Knowledge enables men to rule, and, as has been truly said, for the Spirit there is no veil in any kingdom of nature.

Therefore of old was the man who had to pass into the temple of the Mysteries spoken of as the Gnostic, the Knower. And every Initiation means an extension of consciousness, an extension which is gained when one gate lies behind you; and the next gate only opens when the knowledge you have conquered enables you to turn the key in its lock. As you trace on, Initiation after Initiation, you find that in each one the pupil, the aspirant, the Initiate, is admitted to another and higher world, and shows that he is able to wield its powers, to use its influence, and always to seek one object and one alone, that he may become of greater service to his fellow-men and may help those who cannot help themselves to a swifter road of progress, to a shorter way to bliss. For the only justification of gaining knowledge is that you may use it for service; and Those who hold the keys of knowledge will only place them in the hands of anyone when that person has proved himself eager to serve, and has mastered the desires of the lower self imprisoned in the bodies, and surrendered himself to the will of the higher Self that knows no will but God's.

And as we look away from these high Mysteries that are, and that were known in the outer world of the past more than they are today, we find that there were many preparatory Schools, Mysteries of the less real kind, which gradually prepared the pupil for the higher Mysteries, and some of these still exist. There are occult Schools scattered over our world today, and all look up to the one White Brotherhood as that to which they aspire; they pass along many different lines which have been brought down from ancient times, different ways and different methods and different fashions of instruction, but all realize that they are preparing for the real Mysteries, those over which the great Hierarchy presides. And looking back into the past we find that there were many such secondary Mysteries known to exist, although the method of their teaching remains occult or hidden.

We find, for instance, that there was a stage in the evolution of religions, in which the pupils were no longer able at will to leave the outer body and go to the Temple of the Mysteries, where alone the higher Initiation should be given.

Some of you may know that in connection with the Egyptian pyramids there were chambers of Initiation which had no door, for no one might enter there who could not pass through the wall encircling the Temple; such needed no door through which to go, because he came in the subtler body into the presence of the Hierophants of these Mysteries. So in Ireland there are still left some towers which have puzzled antiquarians because there is no way into them; there is no need for a door for the man who has learned to use the subtler bodies, for there is no wall that can exclude him, no door that can be locked against him, nothing that can keep him from going whither he will, nothing which this earth can erect in the way of barriers. So it was the fashion of these Mysteries of old, the grade below the real, just as in the real, that only those who could consciously use the higher bodies could be admitted, that they might pass through to the great Way of Initiation.

But the time came when people could not do that of their own free will, and then another method was used. They were thrown into a mesmeric or hypnotic trance, touched with what was called in Greek antiquity the Thyrsus, a rod at first filled with living fire, the touch of which at once broke the links between the higher and the lower bodies, and set the Spirit free within its subtler vehicle in full consciousness of that higher life.

So you will find sometimes, in ancient fresco or in ancient sculpture, a priest stands holding in his hand a rod and on the top of the rod a cone. It was a form of the Rod of Power which was used, and was passed along the spinal column up to where that enters the head; as the fiery rod passed up the spinal column the subtler body was drawn together and gradually followed the rising rod until, as it touched the head, the body passed out through the skull and then was set free to reach the subtler worlds. And a little later still that power has been lost, as the world is going on its onward way, deeper and deeper into matter. Then only the astral vision is opened and the astral hearing, and living pictures are shown in subtler matter, which image out the realities of the other worlds. No longer the subtler world is traversed, only a picture of that world is shown; but a living picture, giving much of knowledge, and even down to our own days that is a common way of teaching. When the living pictures made by the great Teachers are thus shown, we have past history reproduced; when the great work of building worlds is imaged in the subtler matter of the astral plane, the pupil studies these pictures as they unroll before him, and understands better than words could tell him the reality of that history of the past.

Then, coming still lower down, as even this power was lost by those who were the Hierophants of the Mysteries, there came a stage that you may read of among the Greeks, when that which was to be taught was shown by acting, and not either in the worlds themselves or in the living pictures that imaged them out; when men were taught to act scenes which continued the lessons which had to be learned; when the astral world was shown as a dramatic scene; when the passions were imaged as animals, and when men clothed in animals' skins and wearing animal masks surrounded the candidate for the Mysteries, endeavored to drive him back, and tried to terrify him. And if within him there was the germ of any vice remaining, then that inner traitor in the citadel of the mind answered to the threat without which was made by the actor who was acting the vice, and the man, terrified, seeing the vice figured as it were in an outer form, shrank back and dared not face his enemy, and so failed in his passage through this test which was to try the purity of the candidate.

So these Mysteries went on right into Christian days, and if you will read your early Christian books, read the writings of the Apostolic Fathers, trace them on from those who were the pupils of the Apostles themselves and through succeeding writers, read St. Clement of Alexandria, read the works of Origen so far as we have them, you will find in the early days of Christianity there were the Mysteries, the real Mysteries of Jesus. There were two lines of instruction; there were first the teachings of those who had been instructed, as both Origen and St. Clement write, by word of mouth, in the secret teachings given by the Christ while He lived and worked amongst men. You remember He said to His Apostles: "Unto you it is given to know the Mysteries of the Kingdom of God, but to others in parables". And the modern Church is content with the parables, and does not seem to feel the lack of the inner teachings which explain the Mysteries of God. And those which were received by tradition, handed down from mouth to ear by generation after generation of worthy and saintly men, those formed the first teachings in the Mysteries, the teachings, as Origen said, given in secret by Christ to His own disciples.

Then there were higher Mysteries, where not human but superhuman lips taught the secrets of the higher worlds, and you find St. Ignatius of Antioch — I think it is, or perhaps Irenaeus — declaring that the Angels were the teachers in those early Christian Mysteries, superhuman beings who came to those who had been instructed in the knowledge handed down from mouth to ear, and who were worthy to receive that higher teaching, and to come into direct touch with those denizens of higher worlds. So was it also in Greece and in Egypt, where those whom Christians call Angels, but whom the older religions spoke of as the Shining Ones, were the teachers and revealed the Mysteries of the higher worlds.

Christianity, as much as any other ancient faith, had Mysteries at the back of the outer religion. Men were baptized into the Christian Church, they passed onwards to the Communion, thus utilizing the outer forms which the Christ had left for the helping of believers. But you may remember how St. Paul declared: "We speak wisdom among those who are perfect", declaring that he did not give the higher teaching to those whom he said, although baptized and communicating Christians, were only babes in Christ. All this passed away; and yet not wholly, for ever the true Mysteries remained; but this difference there was, at least in the western world: there was no open road to the Mysteries, there were no intermediate Schools in which men and women might be instructed — only traditions that such things were or had been; and only here and there was a man, who, having been taught personally and individually, grew strong enough to find his own way to those ever- existing Mysteries of the true Brotherhood of the Masters of the Wisdom. But here and there we still find groups of study. You may trace them through old and Middle Age literature, and one word I may give you as a key, for you will often come across it and perhaps not understand quite what it means When you find among some old books a book which is called a Rosary, you have the name by which the secret books were marked out right through the Middle Ages, in which the alchemist and the astrologer and the searcher after secret wisdom wrote down in glyph and symbol the truths that he knew but dare not openly teach. For we are coming to the days of persecution, when men dared not say the things they knew for fear the exoteric faith should crush them, and the carnal knowledge should destroy the spiritual truth. But still here and there a group is to be found, for never was the succession quite destroyed even upon the earth; but men did not know where to look, they searched far and wide and found not a teacher. For they who knew dreaded to communicate their knowledge, lest the pupil should only be a spy or a traitor, and should betray the Knowers to death. And you know the terrible tragedy of the Templars — they who had some knowledge of the hidden Mysteries — for under torture there were some who declared fragments of knowledge which were used to condemn. You remember how under torture it was declared more than once that when a Templar was initiated into the Mysteries he had to tread upon the Cross, and this was condemned as a sign of blasphemy, it was taken as a sign of unbelief. It was really the sign that the man relied upon the Cross to raise him up to knowledge, and if his feet for a moment were set upon it, it was in order that the Cross might rise with him upon it, and so carry him upon it, and so carry him upwards to a purer air, where some of the lower Mysteries were revealed. And one way of symbolism, and one great body which has come down from those days of the disappearance of the Mysteries, though most of its brethren know not what they possess — they know symbols only but seldom know the reality which these symbols express to the wise — is the great Brotherhood of Freemasonry, scattered over the world, who have kept in symbol what they have lost in knowledge, in order that they, in the days when knowledge returns, may bear testimony that it has never entirely passed away from earth. And those who belong to that Brotherhood will understand what I mean when I say that the treading on the Cross was no outrage, but the entrance over the threshold of knowledge.

And we find as we look backwards that there was a day when Christian Rosenkreuz came from the East to Europe and founded the first open Rosicrucian Society. I call it "open" because it is known to history, though foolish people think that it is myth and not history, forgetting that often myth and legend are the history of the great truth that lies behind. For he was a disciple of the Wisdom sent out by the Brotherhood to bring back the light of knowledge to Europe, and it was from that early Rosicrucian Society that the twelve brethren went out who brought back to Europe the bases of science, who brought alchemy and through that made chemistry possible, who taught astrology and so led on to astronomy, laying the bases of the modern knowledge. For real knowledge begins in the subtler and comes down to the denser world, and it does not begin in the denser and climb upwards to the subtler. And from that day began the re-dawn of science in Europe, and the possibility of knowledge gradually and slowly spreading. You can trace onwards Society after Society, all connected, though bearing different names, and ever teaching the same teachings — the preparation of Europe for the Restoration of the Mysteries in the wider and more effective fashion.

Then you come to the seventeenth and eighteenth centuries, where you have that mysterious Being the Comte de Germain, and where you find him working with our H. P. B., then a member of a great Austrian family still known by the name of Zimsky. You see those two brethren, disciples of the great Lodge, working along hand-in-hand that Europe might grow in knowledge. Then you come to a barrier that was set; for they were trying to change things by knowledge, and the knowledge came into the hands of those not yet fitted to receive it, and the starvation of the people and the misery of the nations, the tyranny and the suffering and the corruption both in Church and State, those were too strong for the teachers who where endeavoring in the world to guide men to knowledge, and the great outburst of the French Revolution poured forth a stream of blood which prevented further teaching along the inner lines. But still to some, here and there, it came, until the day dawned when those same teachers, brethren of the past, began again their work. That which failed in the eighteenth century was begun, in the nineteenth, and the bases of the Theosophical Society were laid and worked for by them, one hidden — for He had passed over the threshold into Masterhood and no longer worked openly among men — and the other, that noble Russian woman, H. P. Blavatsky, to whom the Theosophical Society owed its foundation and still largely owes its life. Then began the preparation for the Restoration of the Mysteries. And then that Brother whom a Master spoke of as "the Brother whom you know as H. P. B. but we otherwise"

34

— he began again, by making a preparatory School within the Society, to lay the foundation of the Mysteries which later will be fully restored in our midst.

For then again, for the first time since from Europe they disappeared, the open way was shown whereon men might walk, and this Theosophical Society of ours, pointing to the Masters who founded it, pointing to the School made by Their messenger, shows the way along which the pupil may begin to walk, until he comes to the gateway of the true Mysteries; the way again is proclaimed and the Teachers are ready to teach.

Once more did the cry go out over the outer world, which you may read in Hindu Scripture: "Awake, arise, seek the great Teachers and attend; for the road, it is said, is narrow and sharp as the edge of a razor." That cry has gone out again, and there are ears to hear, ears that are able to hear the call, lips ready to answer. So in our days and our time, in the many nations of this mortal world, pupils are being found, pupils are being trained, in order that gradually it may be possible to restore the Mysteries as they were in the past, the gateways to the true Mysteries of the Brotherhood.

There you have the inner side of this great movement to which you all belong; and if you look upon the outer world you will see that, in many ways and along many lines, forces are being sent out to prepare the minds of the people at large for a higher and a more spiritual view of life, for a deeper and therefore truer view of human nature. For do not think that the influence of the Masters is limited within the limit of our Theosophical Society; that is Their messenger to the world, the vessel that They have chosen, into which They have poured Their Life; but far over the world Their Life also extends; for just as you may gather together in a reservoir water which shall then be taken from the reservoir and sent far and wide among

35

the people who need it, so it is with this Life; as the rain comes down from the clouds over the whole earth, and not only into the reservoir made to receive a store of waters, so does the Masters' Life pour over the world at large, although concentrated here in the reservoir of the Theosophical Society.

It is our glory that we know how we are working; it is our privilege to be self-conscious co-operators in the working out of the Plan that the Masters are laboring to bring about successfully upon our earth. But we never dare to limit Them nor Their power, Their love nor Their compassion, and They can bring people whence They will, although an open way today is shown whereon surely They will be found.

And so, friends, I who have been bidden speak this word to all nations of the earth, speaking to you who are members of this Society that is Their servant in the lower world, I would say to you, that great are the possibilities that are being unveiled before you, great the avenues of progress which lie open before you today. It is true that you may come into the Society without any belief in the Masters of the Wisdom. It is true that you need not accept any doctrine, reincarnation, karma, or anything else, before you are admissible to the Society. That is true; but also it is true that there are those who know, those who are sent to do this work, those have a right to speak of what they know, and to repeat in the lower world what they have heard in the worlds beyond the physical.

And so it is that the road is open. The outer gate is wide and all who will may enter in. But to the Mysteries it is not so: straight is the gate and narrow is the way that leadeth unto Life Eternal and few there be that find it. Few at present, but to be more and more numerous as years go on; few today, but to increase to many in the days to come.

For there are great forces pouring down upon our world; the gates of the heavenly world are open, and life and power pour down upon the world of men. Well is it for you that your karma has brought you to birth in these happy days; well for you to be in them; but a thousand-fold the better, if within you the intuition which is the voice of the Spirit speaks, so that you may answer to the call of the Masters and find your way to Their feet.

Symbolism of the Equilateral Triangle

by Lydia Bell

The triangle holds its place as a symbol in the mathematics of ideal proportions. As a symbol in ethics it at once suggests the idea of mathematical exactness and method in connection with spiritual problems. A true spiritualism is able to demonstrate its position in the exactness of the law of pure mathematics. A spiritualism that fails in this, fails in the only method known to finite comprehension as exact, and leads to the inference, that a law can express more than the lawgiver. The law of mathematics holds our highest concept of absolute Truth. The law is universal, and in its unfolding gives us the highest possible relation. Music, art, poetry, all that we know of the ennobling and beautifying expressions of the soul, manifest themselves in numbers. The truth of music is in measure; the truth of art is in proportion; the truth of poetry is in ratio. Science has never revealed anything but a broader application of the law of number. Chemistry is combination or addition. Botany is analysis or subtraction. In astronomy we strike the true because the incomprehensible — we deal with the unknown quantity. The true basis of reasoning is from cause to effect. To correctly measure the force of a stream we will go to its source. When the source is unknown, it becomes the unknown quantity of our calculation, and through the application of it as an unknown quantity, we approximate to a true knowledge of it. In dealing with the greatest of all problems — that of existence — mathematical principles have been ignored. I know it is objected that mathematics are too cold for religion. We want the warmth of sentiment and emotion in spiritual things. The warmth of sentiment and emotion, unsupported by the truth of mathematics, is the song without music, poetry without rhythm, and art without harmony. It abides where music, poetry and art have not yet become the language of the soul. As compared to the warmth derived from a mathematical basis, it is the flash of light reflected from a mirror as distinguished from the direct glow of a sunbeam; one scorches and dazzles, the other warms; one blinds the vision, the other is a "lamp to the feet," revealing the way. A change in the multiplication table to suit the fancy of every one who had a problem to solve, would make a chaos of all calculation — without an exact basis in ethics this is our condition in spiritual things. One man's revelation is not another's; and each holds his opinion, or sentiment, as truth. One man's opinions or any set of men's opinions cannot alter the truth as discovered in mathematics. Here and here only, can we determine the problem of life in the terms of law. Here we reach a solution that brings us to the recognition of brotherhood in spiritual things, as we are a recognized brotherhood in mathematics. The axioms of truth have no more to be changed in dealing with the realities of life, than in dealing with its grosser calculations. A universal brotherhood finds its realization in the universal recognition of a Deity that appeals to all in the harmony of an everywhere manifested law.

Starting with the triangle as the unit of all subjective operations our conception of it is based upon our knowledge of the objective unit: we proceed from a knowledge of the part to a concept of the whole — or unknown unit. To do this we transmute the objective to the subjective and raise the power of the numeral to infinity. When thus raised to the power of the infinite unit the triangle is our symbol for truth. As a symbol for the whole of truth, it holds the key to all science, to all wisdom, and its study leads with certain steps to and through that door wherein the mystery of life ceases to be a problem, and becomes revelation. An understanding of the triangle depends upon the analysis of the objective unit, the arithmetic definition of which is "a single thing." The first idea we get from this single thing is wholeness; nothing can be added to it nor subtracted from it without impairing its unity as a single thing. Second: Its unity involves the idea that it can be separated, that it consists of parts. Third: These parts hold certain unchanging relationship to each other, then as related to its wholeness it has unity, as related to its separableness it has diversity, and as related to its unchangeableness it has identity; unity, diversity and identity, are the essential qualities of every "single thing," or every unit, and the equilateral triangle is the symbol that manifests these three qualities in unity. The figure 3 does not do it as we lose in it the idea of three related parts. Three separate 1's will not do it, as the idea of unity is lost. We combine the three to express the unity and diversity, and when combined we have the idea of identity, and the triangle is the symbol of the subjective unit. Each side of the triangle is the figure 1, and this manifests unity in its wholeness, diversity in its two ends and identity in its central point, which is changeless for every figure 1. Thus the figure 1 manifests the triangle in the symbol and the first deduction we make is: *the unit is a trinity.* The triangle is a unit, each part of the triangle is a unit, hence, it follows that *every part manifests the whole.* Seen in motion the triangle measures the arc of the pendulum, these successive arcs make the circle and the circle marks Infinity — or the pendulum swing that marks eternity in space and time, and so annihilates space and time. This idea of the unit in connection with motion and form gives the idea of motionless and formless as manifested truth. Form and motion involve change, the unit cannot change. The magnetic needle in its perfect poise illustrates what I mean, and shows: the motion of the unit in positive or centrifugal, in negative or centripetal, and poise. *Perfect poise is changeless.* The absolute is always the center, a change in the center belongs to finite perception and not to Infinite Truth. The unknown quantity of Infinite Poise will always be the unknown quantity, but as the part manifests the

41

whole we shall always have a measure of understanding proportioned to our discernment. As we do not hold the center, we do not hold both the positive and negative, and so we manifest a minus quantity in all our thinking. The *symbol cannot change*. Its action in truth is *Energy in Poise*. Delsarte makes a clear exposition of this principle. Perfect expression in music is vibrating harmony, and then music is soundless. The human form is the prophecy of the principle in limbs — or positive, head — negative and torso — poise, the hand manifests it in fingers, palm and thumb, the thumb indicates the line of physical balance, and falls when the balance is lost.

Blood, bone, and breath, circulation, secretion and respiration: all functional activity shows us the symbol. We have it in the planet as water-centrifugal, earth-centripetal, and air-poise, or manifested as liquid, solid and gas. It expresses the law of chemical affinity and the organic cell. Light, electricity and magnetism are its etherealized exponents. Of the three primary colors, blue is the life or centrifugal ray, yellow is the illuminating or centripetal ray and red is the warm or poised ray. The ideal of these rays is blue for life or will, yellow for wisdom, and red for love, which brings us to the Divine Father principle, the Divine Mother principle, and the Divine Guild as the Divine Trinity of manifested truth, or the circle of manifested Deity. The nearer man approaches a form that manifests *Energy in Poise,* the nearer he is to taking his place in the line of the triangle. In expression, voice is centrifugal or going out, gesture is poised or within, and the word is concentered or coming back, and this is the order manifested in the child. We reach true expression in proportion as the energy of going out is at one with the energy of coming back: in other words when the impulse of the creature in aspiration is one with the Creator in inspiration, man finds himself a part of the line of the triangle, a part of the word that "in the beginning was God." To express the truth of the triangle, is to

42

manifest the supreme energy of the universe, and that means the bringing of the line of life in ourselves into the line of truth in ourselves. This is the true work of existence. Love measures the poise, *and we know when we have attained it.* There is no room for finding fault, for recrimination or judgment of our neighbor, the battle is with the self.

Some Psychic Experiences

by Edith Wheeler

In thinking over the psychic experiences which have formed a part of my own life, my mind goes back to my childhood's days when I was a little girl of five or six years of age.

I remember a big nursery in an old house in County Tyrone in which two little cribs stood side by side, and over in a corner was the nurse's bed with the cradle beside it in which the baby slept.

I see as clearly as if it were yesterday the room, the places of the cribs, the old-fashioned low cradle on rockers, the position of the windows and the door.

I can remember distinctly one night how I lay awake after the others had gone asleep. I recall how I saw the door, which was ajar, pushed open and a large deerhound came and went across the floor to where the baby lay. I remember how I held my breath as I saw it bend over the cradle and lick the face of the sleeping child. Then I recollect how it crawled under the nurse's bed and disappeared from my sight.

I remember how I cried out in alarm, how the nurse got up most unwillingly, and how she slapped me for telling stories when no trace of the animal could be found.

It was all my imagination, she said, for there was no deer hound in the room, and none about the place.

She hushed me at last to sleep, but I heard her repeat the tale to a neighbor next day, and how that good woman remarked that the baby was bound to grow up a lucky child and to attain high honor. It is not always that one's superstitions are translated so comfortably!

My mother came of a family in which many psychic occurrences had happened. She has often related to me how the sound of a gun was heard going off in the hall of the house before my grandfather's death, and she also relates how her mother, who had died many years before, sat by her bedside during the most critical period of a severe illness. Her presence by her bedside calmed and comforted her, and from that time her recovery was certain.

Another story which my mother very often related to us children was an event connected with her own childhood.

She spent a great deal of her time at the house of an uncle who owned some property, on which was a large and extensive lake.

One day as she walked with her uncle by the water, holding his hand, she was startled to hear the sound of most beautiful music wafted, it seemed to her, from the little island which lay in the center of the lake.

It sounded like a small orchestra of the most delicately stringed instruments, with which were mingled the strains of the harp.

She stopped and drew her uncle's attention to the music, conscious of it all the while, but he could hear nothing.

They turned and walked homewards, and as they drew near to the house her uncle stooped, and said to her, "Do not say anything about the music to your aunt, dear child!"

She said nothing about it at the time, but shortly after a member of the family died and she heard one of the country-folk relate that there was wont to be a warning before one of them died, music or something, but that no one seemed to have heard anything this time.

In the same family "a wee woman" was said to appear at any critical juncture in the family history, and it was only the other day I heard an old family retainer relate the most natural conversations between herself and the same "wee woman."

On one occasion the wee woman had told her how a pot of gold was hidden in a certain field on the property, but as the field had been sold to another, she had not mentioned it, but was sure she could conduct anyone to the spot if they wished to investigate the matter.

As a great deal of money was buried during the troubled times in Irish history, it is quite possible that there is some truth in the matter.

A little niece of my husband while quite a small child of three or four had a phantom playmate whom she called "Frane." Her mother used to discover her in a room playing quite happily with this little child of her imagination. Very often she would say, "Frane would not like to play this," if some game were suggested.

Her mother took her quite seriously and did not show her that she thought there was anything peculiar about the situation, and "Frane" disappeared gradually on the advent of a little baby sister who occupied her attention.

I was telling this story to a friend, and she immediately began to relate how her own little girl, then aged ten, used to play with an imaginary kitten in the same way. The kitten was, however, quite real to her, and she would throw a ball of wool for it to play with, and used to laugh over its attempts to catch it. Also, when going upstairs, she would say, "Mother, do be careful. Can't you see kitty is on that step!" or, "Mother, how can you tramp on kitty's tail?"

Her mother did not talk about this to anyone and made no comment upon it, and the kitten also disappeared gradually when other playmates took its place. This same little girl always associated the people she knew with different colors. Her mother told me of this, and said I could ask her about it myself if I did not allow the child to think the gift was at all peculiar. The child told me that she always saw people's names written across a band of color, but as I questioned her I found it was really not the name but the personality which she connected with colors.

On being asked what color my name "Edith" suggested, she said violet. After a while, when I asked her what her "Aunt Edith" was, she said "yellow," thus showing that the name did not present the color she thought of, but the personality. I have often thought that she was unconsciously looking at our "auras" and giving an impression of what she saw.

When I last saw her, she was a girl of fifteen and had been to school. Her mother said she had not heard her speak of this at all recently. At the time I speak of she was a little girl of ten or eleven.

I had a letter yesterday from a friend in Scotland who has herself great powers of clairvoyance which she always told me were inherited from her grandmother. In the letter she wrote:

"You will be sorry to hear granny is dead; she was always so sweet, I shall miss her very much. Some days before her death she told my aunt who was nursing her that something was going to happen on January 24.

" 'Something nice, I am sure,' said my aunt; 'a nice letter or a present from some one.'

" 'No, dear, not that,' she said; 'something else, you will see.'

"Granny died on January 24. I always told you she had clairvoyance, did I not?"

I feel in honor, bound to admit that often one dreams of dates and seems to have a warning when nothing happens, but then one does not know what might have happened if the warning had not been regarded.

I remember two years ago my mother told me she had awakened to see the date "September 3" very distinctly written before her eyes.

As it happened, we were all on the move at the time, some of us in Scotland for a wedding, while the others had all intended to be doing something specially that day. Two of my brothers gave up their sailing for the day out of respect to our mother's wishes, and the others all stayed indoors at the places where they were. Nothing really happened, but it is possible that an accident might have occurred. A very sudden squall came over the Lough during the afternoon, and some of the boats belonging to the club in which my brothers were members were upset. It is quite possible that if they had been sailing that day they would have been overturned also.

Last year I had a very distinct dream myself; I awakened hearing a voice say slowly and distinctly, "Beware of gourds and lightning on the 28th of February."

I marked the date, which was some weeks ahead, upon the calendar, and refused an invitation for the day. I was careful not to eat anything of the gourd order, and I wondered how I could possibly guard against lightning.

To my relief there was no thunderstorm on the day, but next morning a friend who had been chaffing me unmercifully on the subject of my superstitions told me that some overhead electric wires belonging to the tramway system had fallen on a street which I should most likely have passed over had I been out. Of course, this is a purely speculative theory, but I felt there might be something in the warning against "lightning" after all.

While I am on the subject of dreams, I may tell a story which a great friend of mine who has had many experiences relates.

She was in America at the time, and a voyage home had been arranged with her father and sister. Some business arrangements intervened, and the voyage was postponed. One night she had a curious dream, and the next day she said to her sister, "I believe I am going to England after all. I dreamed I was on board a great steamer; I was by myself; the weather was rough, and I was in the cabin. I remember how a great wave came, shaking the vessel, and how it threw me against the velvet cushions in the saloon. I remember the feel of the velvet, and I found myself being assisted to my feet by a gentleman with side whiskers and a good-humored face. I somehow think I shall go the voyage."

Some days after it was decided that my friend should cross the ocean alone, and that her father and sister should join her later. She had been in bad health, and it was thought wise that she should not postpone the voyage.

One day it was very stormy and the ship lurched, and she was thrown against the cushions in the manner of her dream, and quite naturally she felt herself being assisted to her feet by the exact counterpart of the man of her dream. She afterwards married him, but of course that is not a part of the story.

This same friend told me a very clear account of clairaudience which she had experienced. Two friends of hers, a doctor and his wife, had gone to London on a visit, and were expected home on a certain day. She called upon this day to bid them welcome back, but found they had not arrived. On her way to her own house she heard a voice say very distinctly, "The family is not coming back to live here; they are going to *stay* in London." She related this to her husband as a matter of fact. Next day, the family patriarch, a doctor, came around and asked to see her husband, also a doctor, and they went into the study to have a chat.

"I just wanted to tell you," said the doctor , "that we are not coming back to live here, I have bought a practice…"

"Oh, I knew that," said the other, "You are going to stay in London."

"Impossible that you should know," said the doctor, "we have told no one."

"Well, well," said the other, "My wife told me yesterday." When my friend was interrogated and acknowledged how she knew, there was some consternation and surprise, but the fact remained, it was true.

An intimate friend of mine, a doctor, told me of a strange occurrence which had happened to himself. He was on board a steamer on which he had gone a voyage, as ship's doctor, and while there had a very violent attack of malarial fever which he had contracted abroad.

One day the stewardess, who was a Roman Catholic, related to him that during his illness she had come into his cabin to find him out of bed and officiating at what she declared to be the service of the Sacrament in the Roman Catholic Church.
    When relating this, she said, "I did not know you were a Roman Catholic, doctor,"

"I am a Protestant," my friend replied, "and I have never even seen the service which you describe in any Roman Catholic church."

When relating this story afterwards, the doctor used to laugh and say, "I wonder is that a proof that I was a Roman Catholic priest in some other life; certainly I never saw the service in a chapel!"

A story which is often related in the bosom of the family is one which we call "The Obstinate Man."

My father is the hero of the story, and no one laughs more over the relation of the incident than himself.

Among country people in the North of Ireland there is a great feeling against any one making a horse go anywhere when the said horse has shown a decided disinclination to move. Of course, there are certain obstinate animals which are lazy and never want to go on anywhere. But when an otherwise well-behaved horse suddenly stops short, plants its feet well in front and refuses to go forward, the Ulster countryman decides it is best not to urge it.

The scene of my story is the high road which leads from Ballywilliam, along the Warren into the town of Donaghadee. My parents often leased a little roadside cottage with a garden for us children for the summer months, and very often my father would sit of a Saturday afternoon in the garden reading his newspaper.

As he was sitting thus one afternoon, he noticed that a horse and cart suddenly stopped at the gate and did not move on. It was a cart on which was a load of hay, and on the top was an old man holding the reins and an old woman clasping a bundle. Both seemed to have fallen asleep, or at least were quite motion less. The horse stood still too.

"Now then, my good people, what do you want?" said my father politely.

"Nothing, sir, nothing," replied the old man, also very politely, and my father retired again to his seat.

Time went on; at least a quarter of an hour had passed when my father thought he would venture the question again.

"Can I do nothing to help you?" he inquired.

"No, no," said the old woman. "You can do nothing. The old mare has stopped of herself, and here we bide."

"What!" exclaimed my father. "Stuff and nonsense, I never heard of such folly. Here you bide all night, maybe, if the lazy beast won't move."

"Perhaps," said the old man quietly, showing little interest in the matter.

"I'll soon make her go," said my father, as he seized the reins. But the old mare stood immovable.

"You see thon," said both together. "Thon" in the North of Ireland means more than one would think.

"I see nothing," answered my father, now thoroughly angry, and seizing a bucket of water which lay near he threw it over the mare and so startled the beast that it started forward at a trot.

My father withdrew to the garden, triumphant!

Scene II in my story took place further along the road at a spot which is called "The Warren Wall;" on one side of the road is a long stretch of a high wall, on the other a ditch.

A sister of mine was plodding along the road from Donaghadee when she reached the top of a hill and saw a country cart come towards her drawn by a white horse, an old couple sitting on the top of the load.

Suddenly with cries and shrieks a holiday crowd upon a coach bore down upon them, and before she could speak crash went the coach into the cart, and the old man and woman were hurled into the ditch.

She ran to their assistance, found them fairly intact, though terribly shaken, and insisted on them returning to her home to get something to do them good.

Nothing loth, the old couple agreed, turned the cart, and limped back.

My sister stopped at the cottage gate, and hearing some little fuss my father appeared from the garden.

"My goodness!" said the old woman, "it's the obstinate man!"

It was indeed. My father has never lost that title, and when we want to make him feel that there may be something in a superstition after all, we remind him of the old mare and the old couple who thought the mare knew more about it than he did that day at all events.

Was it animal foresight or only a strange coincidence?

In Madame Blavatsky's great tome, the *Secret Doctrine*, we find the following passage: *Kriyashakti—that mysterious power of thought which enables it to produce external, perceptible, phenomenal results by its own inherent energy. The ancients held that any idea will manifest itself externally if one's attention and will is deeply concentrated upon it.*

In another part of the book, it reads: *Kriyashakti— that mysterious and divine power, latent in the will of every man, which, if not called to life, quickened and developed by Yoga training, remains dormant in 999,999 cases out of a million and becomes atrophied.*

Now I wonder was the following story the result of Kriyashakti?

My husband and I were alone in the house one Sunday evening, when he was taken with a very severe shivering attack which I felt was the prelude of an acute illness.

Almost at that moment a friend called at the house, and I asked him to lose no time in going for the doctor who lived at some distance, quite twenty minutes' walk away.

My husband got into bed, and despite all remedies which I could think of, the shivering continued.

As I stood by his bedside, I remember thinking how foolish it was not to have asked my friend to stay with my husband while I mounted my bicycle and rode for the doctor. It would have been so simple, and would have taken much less time. My mind was intent on the folly of not having gone on my bicycle myself. I may here explain that at that time ladies' bicycles were few and far between; it was quite out of the ordinary to see a lady ride, and most extraordinary to meet one riding a bicycle on Sunday. The place where we lived was very old-fashioned in this respect, and bicycling on Sunday was considered most unsuitable.

My friend returned with the doctor, and as my husband's illness was severe I was not out of the house for some days.

When I was able to be out I called at my mother's house to tell her of my husband's illness.

"Of course, we knew on Sunday evening that something was wrong," she said, "as I was standing with your sister at the

56

window and we saw you ride past on your bicycle. Some thing must be wrong, your sister said, and you must be going for the doctor. Of course, we knew you would not be riding your bicycle otherwise."

"What did I wear?" I said.

"Oh, you had on your grey dress and your pink hat; I expect you were in a hurry."

I have always felt that in my anxiety and with my concentrated thought on going on the bicycle I must have appeared to my own people on that machine and in the grey dress and pink hat which was my Sunday afternoon attire, but certainly not my bicycle outfit.

There is really nothing uncommon or remarkable in any of these facts which I have related, but they may go to swell the number of authentic instances of the spirit of an animal being seen, warnings of death, clairaudience, true dreams, clairvoyance, animal foresight, and ghosts of the living.

Most of the people mentioned are living and could be interrogated on the subjects mentioned if necessary, for I have been careful only to relate facts which have come under my own experience or incidents which I have heard related over and over again by friends interested in getting any authentic information on these subjects, and whose accounts I know to be perfectly genuine.

A Cumberland Witch

by Mrs. J Allsopp

I have been asked by some friends interested in occult subjects to record some information which came to me in my youth, as likely to prove interesting to others. The facts narrated were told to me by my grandmother, who had personally known the author of the proceedings.

About a hundred years ago near the small town of Brampton, in Cumberland, lived a woman who went by the name of Nanny. She was supposed by the country-folk to be a witch, and to have the power to ill-wish and overlook. The people stood in great awe of her and treated her with a fearful respect. Some envied her powers, others conciliated her as much as possible. She was the usual referendum when things were lost, and could always tell where they were. It chanced that my grandfather, who kept a large dairy farm, had for some time been annoyed by the loss of his butter firkins. This became more and more frequent, and as he could not catch the thief, he decided to seek Nanny's aid in the matter. A neighbor offered to accompany him, as he was rather nervous. As they approached her dwelling she came out and called to my grandfather before he had the chance to speak, "Don't come any farther, the man who has your firkins is with you." And it turned out to be true. The man had the firkins.

She was of a rather peculiar appearance, and a less terrible person than she would have been subjected to ridicule. It happened one day that she was going past a farm where the maidens were washing in the open air. As she passed, they laughed at her. She stopped, came back and said: "Ye may laugh and dance till I choose ye to stop." And they began to laugh and dance, and nothing would make them cease. At last in desperation their master went to the old woman and prayed her on bended knees to forgive the girls. This she did, but they had danced twenty-four hours.

It is said that she once entered a house and all the doors both upstairs and down flew violently open. She is supposed to have uttered many prophecies. Her most famous one is that regarding an important local family. This was: that when the church bell should toll without hands in the town church, and the hare litter on the hearth-stone, great misfortune would happen to them. This did actually come to pass. The church, fallen into ruins almost, gave free ingress to the cattle, and a cow got in and caught her horns in the bell rope, causing the bell to ring. At their ancestral home, a hare got into a disused room and littered on the hearth. Strange as it may seem, a long period of misfortune ensued.

I have said that her power was envied by some. A girl who had watched her very closely for some time, greatly desired to be as clever as she was. She met her one day and plucked up courage to tell her so. "All right, lass," said the old dame, "come to my cottage tonight, at midnight and see; thou tell no one, and thou shalt be as clever as I am." Greatly elated, the girl determined to do as she was bidden, and at midnight sought the lonely cottage of Nanny. She entered shrinkingly, but Nanny assured her there was nothing to fear. Then she asked the girl if she *really* meant what she had said that afternoon. Nanny was assured that she did. "Well then," said Nanny, "put thy hand on thy head and the other under thy foot and say 'All's the Devil's,' and thou must *really* mean it." There was a terrific burst of thunder, and the girl fled in terror from the cottage. This story about the girl had a very weird effect on me. When I retired that night, it seemed that someone stood by the bed and urged me to repeat Nanny's words. It became a terrible strife of wills and lasted all night. I insisted on saying "All's the Lord's." It passed with the day, but in the morning the bed was saturated with perspiration, and for many years after I dared not sleep alone. How can these things be accounted for?

Many are the tales still current in the country-side about Nanny. The day she died there was the most awful thunder storm ever known in those parts. The lightning ran along the ground and the thunder was terrific. She is buried in the tiny churchyard of the old Saxon church of Denton, near Carlisle.

Allegory of the Cup

by Katherine Hillard

When Rabelais' hero, Pantagruel, has completed the long and toilsome voyage of discovery that he makes for the benefit of his friend Panurge, the two arrive at last at the shrine of the Divine Bottle, to which they are guided by the illustrious Lantern, emblem of the light of Truth. The whole description of their progress through the underground region in which the temple they seek is built, is full of the symbolism of initiation, through whose manifold tests the travelers are obliged to pass. The mystical seven planets, with their appropriate jewels and metals, are represented here, and the twelve signs of the zodiac, with other astronomical figures, are painted upon the dome over the fountain, which is itself shaped like a heptagon within a perfect circle. From this temple the neophyte, specially arrayed for the ceremony, is conducted to the inner shrine, a round chapel built of transparent stone of richest workmanship. Within it is another seven-angled fountain, in the midst of which stands the Divine Bottle, a pure, oval crystal. The hymn of invocation having been sung, the oracle pronounces the one word *"Drink!"*

And the priestess dismisses the seekers with these words: "Here below, in these circumcentral regions, we establish as the sovereign good, not to take and receive, but to impart and give; and we reckon ourselves happy, not in taking much of others' goods, but in imparting and giving of our own to our fellows. Go, friends, in the protection of that intellectual sphere of which the center is everywhere and the circumference nowhere, that we call God. All philosophers and ancient sages, the more surely and pleasantly to accomplish the road of divine knowledge and the pursuit of wisdom, have esteemed two things necessary — the guidance of God and the love of mankind. Now go, in the name of God, and may He be your guide!"

It is easy to see the identity of this Divine Bottle with the sacred cup or consecrated drink of all nations. The Greek and Roman gods drank from the cup of Hebe or Ganymede (two personifications of the same idea), and the priestesses of their oracles also drank deep draughts of the sacred beverage before they prophesied, as in India the Soma juice still inspires the Brahmin at the altar. In the second Book of Esdras, ch. XIV, Esdras is commanded by a vision to re-write the burnt books of the law, and to prepare him for the task he is told by the Voice, "Open thy mouth, and drink that I give thee to drink." "Then opened I my mouth," says Esdras, "and behold, he reached me a full cup, which was full as it were with water, but the color of it was like fire. And I took it and drank: and when I had drunk of it, my heart uttered understanding, and wisdom grew in my breast, for my spirit strengthened my memory."

In the 2nd volume of Madame Blavatsky's book *Isis Unveiled*, we are told that in the sacred rites of Bacchus (from which the ceremony of the Eucharist was derived) the hierophant-initiator presented symbolically before the final *revelation* wine and bread to the candidate, who partook of both in token that the spirit was to quicken matter, that is, that the divine *Wisdom* was to be revealed to him. And in a note to her book, the *Secret Doctrine*, we read that "Soma is with the Hindus the father, albeit illegitimate, of Buddha Wisdom," that is, that occult knowledge comes from a thorough understanding of lunar mysteries, or, taking Soma as the sacred beverage, that wisdom, "albeit illegitimate," follows the drinking of it.

With the ceremony of the Eucharist and its sacred vessels is closely connected the symbolism of the Holy Grail, the principal *motif* in the legends of King Arthur.

The stories of the Holy Grail are all to be traced back to the legend of St. Joseph of Arimathea, who was said to have brought to Britain from the Holy Land the sacred vessel of the Last Supper. In the French prose romance of the *Saint Grail,* it is said that St. Joseph, having obtained leave from Pilate to take down the body of Jesus from the cross, first went to that upper room where the Last Supper was held, and found there the shallow bowl from which Christ was said to have eaten the paschal lamb with his disciples. And into this cup, as the body was lowered from the cross, fell many drops of blood from the still open wounds. "According to Catholic theology, where the body or the blood of Christ is," points out Mr. Thomas Arnold, "there, by virtue of the hypostatic union, are His soul and His divinity." The Grail therefore becomes a divine marvel and mystery, a worker of miracles and wonders. By the Grail, St. Joseph's life was sustained in prison for forty-two years without food, and from it he imbibed also the food of spiritual wisdom. Wherever we find the symbol of the bowl, the bottle, or the cup, the idea, is expressed or implied of divine wisdom as its contents. So, in Hermes Trismegistus, as translated into French by Menaro, we read: "God did not create all men with Intuition, because he wished to establish it in the midst of the souls of men as a prize to strive for. He filled a great bowl with it, and sent it by a messenger, ordering him to cry to the hearts of men: 'Baptize ye, ye who can, in this bowl; ye who believe that you will return to Him who has sent it, ye who know wherefore you are born!' And those who answered the call, and were baptized in this Intuition, these possess the *Gnosis,* and have become the initiated of the Spirit, the perfect men. Those who did not understand the call possess reason but not Intuition, and know not wherefore and by whom they were formed. Composed alone of passions and desires, they do not admire that which is worthy to be contemplated, but give themselves up to the pleasures and appetites of the body, and believe that this is the end of man. But those who have received the gift of God, judging by their works, O Tat, are immortal, and no longer mortal. They embrace, by intuition, all that is in the earth and in the heavens, and all that there may be above the heavens. Disdaining all things corporeal and incorporeal, they aspire towards the One and the Only. This is the wisdom of the Spirit, to contemplate Divine things, and to know God. This is the blessing of the Divine Bowl."

Sometimes the symbol of the *cup* is transmuted into that of the *well* or *the fountain*. In a note to *Isis Unveiled*, Madame Blavatsky says: "The 'well,' in the kabalistic sense, is the mysterious emblem of the Secret Doctrine." "If any man thirst, let him come unto me and drink," says Jesus (John vii, 38), and therefore Moses, the adept, is represented sitting by a *well*, to which the *seven* daughters of the Priest of Midian come for water. And in the story of the woman of Samaria Jesus sat by a well, and used it as the symbol of spiritual wisdom. "Whosoever drinketh of this water shall thirst again," said Jesus, "but whosoever drinketh of the water that I shall give him shall never thirst; but the water that I shall give him shall be in him a well of water, springing up into everlasting life." (John iv, 13-14.)

As the fountain of Moses had seven priestesses, the fountain of Rabelais seven angles, so the mystic fountain of Boccaccio (in the *Ameto)* is surrounded by seven nymphs, for "Wisdom has rested her house upon *seven* pillars." (Prov. ix, 1.)

When we come down from the symbolism of the Middle Ages to that of modern times, we find the story of the Holy

Grail most beautifully retold by Tennyson. If he has omitted the incident of the drops of blood that fell from the figure upon the cross into the Cup, he has restored another point in the old legends of King Arthur quite as significant, the story of the "Siege perilous" of Merlin, that magic chair that always stood vacant, for Merlin had declared that therein

"No man could sit but he should lose himself."

But Sir Galahad, the maiden knight, burning with desire to find the Holy Grail, caught the true meaning of the oracle, and crying "If I lose myself, I save myself!", sat down in Merlin's chair.

"And all at once, as there we sat, we heard

A cracking and a riving of the roofs,

And rending, and a blast, and overhead

Thunder, and in the thunder was a cry.

And in the blast there smote along the hall

A beam of light seven times more clear than day:

And down the long beam stole the Holy Grail

All over covered with a luminous cloud,

And none might see who bare it, and it past.

But every knight beheld his fellow's face

As in a glory,"

and then it was that all the knights present swore a vow to ride for a year and a day in search of the Holy Grail, because they had seen not itself, but only the cloud that covered it. But Sir Galahad, having "lost himself, to save himself," had seen the Holy Grail descend upon the shrine, and move before him like a blood-red star, to guide his steps. Sir Percival comes up with him as he is nearing the end of his quest, and Sir Galahad bids his friend come with him to watch his departure to the spiritual city. And Sir Percival went, and saw, stretching out across a great morass, an ancient way

"Where, link'd with many a bridge,

A thousand piers ran into the great Sea.

And Galahad fled along them bridge by bridge.

And every bridge as quickly as he crost

Sprang into fire and vanish'd, tho' I yearned

To follow; and thrice above him all the heavens

Opened and blazed with thunder such as seemed

Shoutings of all the sons of God: and first

At once I saw him far on the great Sea,

In silver-shining armor starry-clear;

And o'er his head the holy vessel hung

Clothed in white samite or a luminous cloud.

And with exceeding swiftness ran the boat,

If boat it were — I saw not whence it came.

And then the heavens opened and blazed again

Roaring, I saw him like a silver star —

And had he set the sail, or had the boat

Become a living creature clad with wings?

And o'er his head the Holy Vessel hung

Redder than any rose, a joy to me,

For now I knew the veil had been withdrawn.

Then in a moment when they blazed again

Opening, I saw the least of little stars

Down on the waste, and straight beyond the star

I saw the spiritual city and all her spires

And gateways, in a glory like one pearl —

No larger, tho' the goal of all the saints —

Strike from the sea: and from the star there shot

A rose-red sparkle to the city, and there

Dwelt, and I knew it was the Holy Grail,

Which never eyes on earth again shall see."

In the magazine *Lucifer,* for Oct., 1888, Mr. Ashton Ellis had a fine article on the *Parsifal* of Wagner, whose hero is identical with Tennyson's Sir Percival. Speaking of the Holy Grail, Mr. Ellis says: "Is not this the Divine Wisdom of the ages, the *theosophia* which has been ever jealously guarded by bands of brothers, and to which, in the words of the drama, there leads no path, nor can anyone find it unless it guide his footsteps?" (as Sir Galahad was guided.). . . "Sought by no earthly paths, found by no course of learned study, set in a spot whence Time and Space have fled away, this is the eternal well of changeless truth." And as Mr. Ellis points out, "when the spirit of Love and divine Compassion has conquered the world, then the command shall be 'Unveil the Grail, open the shrine!'"

And, so we come back to the teachings of that great, but grossly-misinterpreted soul, Rabelais, to find that his priestess also declares that the two things necessary to the pursuit of Divine Wisdom are the guidance of God and the love of man. The oracle of the Divine Bottle has but one word to say to the listening soul, — "Drink!"; but is not this one word equivalent to the saying of Jesus, "If any man thirst, let him come unto me and drink"? Both oracles imply the same thing, an effort on the part of the applicant. The water of Wisdom is to be had for the asking; but that "asking" is not a mere formula; it is labor as well as prayer. "To reach Nirvana one must reach self-knowledge," it is stated in Madame Blavatsky's book, the *Voice of the Silence*, "and self-knowledge is the child of loving deeds." Before a man can become a vessel of honor fit for the Master's use, he must have purified himself from all sin, and then the Divine Wisdom will fill his soul.

In studying the words of the seers upon the subject of Intuition, or Spiritual Wisdom, we must remember that the spirit has to do with things of the spirit, not with the concerns of everyday life. When Rabelais' hero first set out in search of the oracle, the question upon his lips related only to the advisability of marriage, but to such queries the oracle gave no response. When Laurence Oliphant felt that "intuition" bade him follow another man as a god, he mistook the nature of intuition, which is not active upon this plane and could take no cognizance of individuals. That is the property of *instinct,* and is but an extension of that faculty of the animal soul that we see developed to such an extent in the likes and dislikes of dogs, for instance. Give to Caesar the things which are Caesar's; do not expect the Divine Spirit to do your fortune-telling, or to direct your daily comings and goings.

There is another source of confusion, sometimes, in the fact that wisdom, or intuition, is spoken of in both an active and a passive sense, as a process and as the result of that process. So, we may think of intuition as the clear light that shines in upon the soul and enables us to see truth, or we may think of it as the sense of vision by which we apprehend that truth. In the teachings of Theosophy we speak of *Buddhi* as a passive principle, the vehicle of Atma, or as an active principle whose vehicle is Manas. All depends upon the point of view; upon whether we begin at the top or at the bottom of the scale. But though, in thinking of the prism, we may think of the yellow as following the green or preceding the orange, we cannot place it between the violet and the red. Instinct may guide the reason, but intuition enlightens the soul. For intuition is one with that Wisdom which is "privy to the mysteries of the Knowledge of God," and "in all ages entering into holy souls, she maketh them friends of God and prophets."

Divine Magic

by Jessie Horne

Magic is Divine Science. A "Great Arcanum" which lies hid within the heart of each — therefore within the reach of whoso will.

Divine Magic is a knowledge of the universe, its laws, and their method of working. This knowledge is no corollary of cut and dried statements, facts gathered up from outside observations of natural phenomena, but a living, realized, being — with nature — an intimate acquaintance with the cause at the back of the effects. It implies such a thorough insight into the working of these laws as will give power to work with them and quicken their effects. Madame Blavatsky says of Magic, — "A thorough familiarity with the occult faculties of everything existing in nature, visible as well as invisible; their mutual relations, attractions and repulsions; the cause of these traced to the spiritual principle which pervades and animates all things; the ability to furnish the best conditions for this principle to manifest itself, in other words a profound and exhaustive knowledge of natural law, this was and is the basis of Magic."

To the magician a miracle in its general acceptance is an impossibility; there is for him no supernatural, but "all wonders are produced by a practical application of the hidden laws of nature." That law which rules the springing up of a field-daisy is the same used by the Magician to cause a seed to germinate, take root, leaf, flower and seed in the space of half an hour; in the first instance nature works unaided, in the second she is sped on her course by a Master Mind; it is the same cause and the same method of working — but quickened.

Nature's secrets are not yielded up easily. Not to the average mind does she make obeisance. The man who approaches her with his outer senses alone, departs as empty as he comes, or filled only with the dry husks of knowledge which is but hearsay and worthless. The voice of Nature speaks only to Soul- man and through the Soul-senses, of which each has a full complement, dormant though they may be in many. To the man of full sense, a new language becomes apparent — a real thing — no mere poet's dream, but a decided distinct fact; so much so that he can practically apply the knowledge gained through it to his outer and everyday life, a knowledge certainly not to be gained by means of book-learning alone (though we must admit that in some cases that is a factor not to be undervalued), but gained through an inward recognition of one's Higher Self as one with the spiritual world, of one's lower self as one with the elemental and phenomenal world, and by the aid of developed inner senses to recognize the operation taking place within each of these.

The elemental world, as a whole, is reflected in our elemental nature — that part over which the higher has charge. The Higher Self reflects the spiritual universe. We, the ego, the cognizer, the middle man, can from this vantage point study the operations of both, draw future knowledge from the higher to supplement and aid the lower elemental being; can recall from the lower stages of evolution through which we have already passed. Thus reviving the pure nature of the lower from experience, wresting wisdom from the higher, the Soul-man — the Magician — becomes a conscious link connecting the two worlds, and affords a field wherein the two may interblend and so produce other states — other races — other universes.

In so far as we help evolution, we are all more or less magicians. But the magician proper is he who is in a position to consciously help towards that end. The strong man is he who has at his finger's ends the history, manners and customs of those small beings who go to make up his body and bodies; who recognizes the strong bond of sympathy which necessarily exists between himself and them; and who further realizes himself as one of the myriad of other beings who in their turn go to make up a greater Soul — and who from such intimate contact with all these lives on all planes of being contains within himself an infallible encyclopedia standing good for all time.

In all ages Divine Magic has been closely connected with the Great Religion presiding over any particular cycle or race. It is the heart and soul of all the systems. The priests and priestesses who presided over the rites and ceremonies were specially trained souls — trained in a knowledge of Man and Nature in their noumenal and phenomenal aspects — trained to a realization and perfect use of their inner senses — trained moreover to know themselves as the Will — the Lords and Masters over themselves — and who, having conquered, stand through successive ages as Invincible Forces silently demonstrating the power of controlled mind. These are the Chaldean Magi — the Hierophants of Egypt — the Initiates of the Greek Mysteries, the Magicians and Gods of all ages. It is they who as Priest-Kings after the order of Melchizedek presided over the lawgiving of kingdoms. It is they who as Priestly Instructors governed the Colleges and Schools and trained the future Teachers — Kings and Law-givers. It is they who in the Great Libraries and Archives guarded vast stores of written knowledge that the combined efforts of the Great Helpers of Humanity had accumulated and given into their keeping. It is they who in all ages protected and still protect the Sacred Truths — the Heirloom of Humanity.

The time is not far off when men will again recognize that a perfect state of society will only be commenced as the high places and offices of the land are in the hands of men perfect in a knowledge and control of themselves — men who consciously from a compassionate sympathy know the needs of humanity as apart from its desires, and who are ready to sacrifice themselves on the altar of self-abnegation that these needs may be met and satisfied. Then will the Schools, the Colleges, the Universities re-become holy places, veritable gardens of pure delight, the delight of the self-conquered Soul exulting in the freedom natural to it; then again will Justice preside over the interests of the peoples, and the selfish and avaricious working for self-aggrandizement feel their power depart, and love and joy rule the nations.

Neither is this so far off. For the cry of humanity is great. The Heart of the Universe unfailingly responds to the call of its children.

Divine Magic will again become a known power in the land, is now actively at work to supply the demand of craving Nature; the Wisdom Religion is weaving still another garment wherein to manifest. Science and Intuition will again grasp hands, and the outer and inner senses of man unite to form a more perfect knowledge of a Perfect Universe.

Alchemy in the Nineteenth Century

by Helena P. Blavatsky

The language of archaic chemistry or Alchemy has always been, like that of the earlier religions, symbolical.

We have shown in the *Secret Doctrine* that everything in this world of effects has three attributes or the triple synthesis of the seven principles. In order to state this more clearly, let us say that everything which exists in the world around us is made up of three principles and four aspects just as we have shown to be the case with man.

As man is a complex unity consisting of a body, a rational soul and an immortal spirit so each object in nature possesses an objective exterior, a vital soul, and a divine spark which is purely spiritual and subjective.

The first of this threefold proposition cannot be denied, the second cannot logically be objected to, for if we admit that metals, certain woods, minerals and drugs possess inherent powers to produce effects on living organisms, then official science practically admits its truth. As for the third, of the presence of an absolute quintessence in each atom, materialism, which deals only with the *anima mundi,* denies it utterly.

Much good may it derive from this agnostic attitude. We for our part, finding in materialism an undoubted proof of the existence of moral and spiritual blindness, make no account of the denial and, leaving the blind to lead the blind, proceed with our subject.

Thus as with natural objects, so every science has its three fundamental principles and may be applied through all three or by the use of only one of them.

Before Alchemy existed as a science its quintessence alone acted in nature's correlations (as indeed it still does) and in all its planes.

When there appeared on earth men endowed with a superior intelligence they allowed this supreme power to have full and uncontrolled action and from it they learnt their first lessons. All that they had to do was to imitate it. But in order to reproduce the same effects by an effort of individual will, they were obliged to develop in their human constitution a power called Kriyasakti in occult phraseology.

This faculty is creative, and is so simply because it is the agent on an objective plane of the first creative principle. It resembles a lightning conductor in that it conducts and gives definite direction to the creative quintessence which otherwise, if led blindly into the lower planes, kills; but which brought down through the channel of the human intellect creates according to a predetermined plan.

From this Alchemy was born; and magnetic magic, and many other branches of the tree of occult science.

When in the course of ages nations grew up so intensely saturated with egotism and vanity as to be convinced of their complete superiority to all others living in the present, or who had lived in the past; when the development of Kriyasakti became more difficult and the divine faculty had almost disappeared from the earth, then they forgot little by little the wisdom of their ancestors. They even went further and rejected altogether the tradition of their antediluvian parents, denying with contempt the presence of a spirit and of a soul in this the most ancient of all sciences. Of the three great attributes of nature they only accepted the existence of matter or rather its illusory aspect, for of real matter or *substance* even the materialists themselves confess a complete ignorance; and truly they are right, nor have they even the vaguest conception of what it is.

Thus there grew up the science of modern chemistry.

Change is the constant effect of cyclic evolution. The perfect circle becomes One, a triangle, a quaternary and a quinary. The creative principle issued from the rootless root of absolute existence, which has neither beginning nor end, and of which the symbol is the serpent or *perpetuum mobile* swallowing its tail in order to reach its head, has become the Azoth of the alchemists of the middle ages. The circle becomes a triangle, emanating the one from the other as Minerva from the head of Jupiter. The circle hypothecates the absolute; the right line issuing from it represents a metaphysical synthesis and the left a physical one. When Mother Nature shall have made of her body a line joining these two, then will come the moment of awakening for the Cosmic Activity. Until then Purush, the spirit, is separated from Prakriti — material nature still unevolved. Its legs exist only in a state of potentiality, and cannot move nor has it arms wherewith to work on the objective forms of things sublunary. Wanting in limits, Purush cannot begin to build until it has mounted into the neck of Prakriti the blind, when the triangle will become the microcosmic star. Before reaching this stage they must both pass through the quaternary state and that of the cross which conceives, this is the cross of earthly mystics, who make a great display of this their beflowered symbol, namely: the cross divided into four parts, which may be read Taro, Ator, and Rota, Tora. The Virgin, or adamic earth substance which was

79

the Holy Spirit of the old Alchemists of the Rosy Cross, has now been changed by the Kabbalists, those flunkeys to modern science, into Na^2Co^3 Kali and C^2H^6O or Alcohol.

Ah! Star of the morning, daughter of the dawn, how fallen from thine high estate — poor Alchemy. All on this ancient planet, thrice deceived, is doomed to tire and, sliding into oblivion, to be destroyed; and yet that which once was, is and shall be forever, even to the end of time. Words change and the meaning underlying them becomes quickly disfigured. But the ideas which are their root and parent shall endure. The ass' skin in which nature's queen wrapped herself in order to deceive fools as in the story of Perrault — for the disciple of the old philosophers will always recognize the truth, no matter under what garb, and will adore it, this ass' skin we must believe is more congenial to the tastes of modern philosophy and materialistic alchemists, who sacrifice the living soul for the empty form, than Royal Nature naked and unadorned. And thus it is that the skin only falls before Prince Charming, who recognizes in the ring sent the marriage betrothal.

To all those courtiers who hover round Dame Nature while cutting at her material envelope, she has nothing to present but her outer skin. It is for this reason that they console themselves by giving new names to old things, old indeed as the world itself, declaring loudly the while that they have discovered something new. The necromancy of Moses has in this way become modern Spiritualism; and the Science of the old initiates of the temple, the magnetism of the gymnosophists of India; the healing mesmerism of Sculapius "the Savior," is only received now on condition that it is called hypnotism, in other words Black Magic under its proper title.

Modern materialists would have us believe that Alchemy or the transmutation of base metals into gold and silver has from the earliest ages been nothing more than charlatanism. According to them it is not a science but a superstition, and therefore all those who believe, or pretend to believe in it, are either dupes or impostors. Our encyclopedias are full of abusive epithets leveled at Alchemists and Occultists.

Now, gentlemen of the French Academie, this may be all very well, but if you are so sure of yourselves, let us have at least some clear and irrefutable proof of the absolute impossibility of the transmutations of metals. Tell us how it is that a metallic base is found even in alkalis. We know certain scientists, men of recognized ability even, who think that the idea of reducing the elements to their first state and even to their primordial essence is not so stupid as it seemed at first sight. Gentlemen, these elements when once you have admitted that they all existed in the beginning in one igneous mass, from which *you* say the earth's crust has been formed, these may be reduced again and brought through a series of transmutations to be once more that which they originally were. The question is to find a solvent sufficiently strong to effect in a few days or even years that which nature has taken ages to perform. Chemistry and, above all, Mr. Crookes has sufficiently proved that there exists a relationship between metals so marked as to indicate not only a common source but an identical genesis.

Then, Gentlemen, I would ask you who laugh at alchemy and alchemists with a mirth bred of a consciousness of superior wisdom, how it is that one of your first chemists, M. Berthold, author of *La Synthese,* deeply read in alchemical lore, is unable to deny to alchemists *a most profound knowledge of matter.*

And again, how is it that M. Chevreul, that venerable sage, whose great age, no less than his living to the last in the full possession of all his faculties, has moved to wonder our present generation, which, with its over-weening self-sufficiency, is so difficult to penetrate or rouse; how comes it, we say, that he who made so many practical and useful discoveries for modern industry, should have possessed so many works on alchemy.

Is it not possible that the key to his longevity may be found in one of these very works, which according to you is but a collection of superstitions as useless as they are ridiculous.

The fact remains that this great savant, the father of modern chemistry, took the trouble to bequeath after his death, to the library of the Museum, the numerous works he possessed on this "false science," and here in this act of his we have an unmistakable revelation of the estimation in which he held them. Nor have we yet heard that those luminaries of science attached to this sanctuary have thrown these books on alchemy into the waste paper basket as useless rubbish full of fantastic reveries engendered by the sick imagination of a diseased brain.

Besides, our wise men forget two things — in the first place never having found the key to these hermetic books, they have no right to decide whether this *jargon* preaches truth or falsehood, and secondly, that wisdom was certainly not born for the first time with them, nor must it necessarily disappear from the world on their demise.

Each science, we repeat, has its three aspects; all will grant that there must be two, the objective and the subjective. Under the first head we may put the alchemical transmutations with or without the powder or projection; under the second we place all speculations concerning the nature of the mind. Under the third is hidden a high and spiritual meaning. Now since the symbols of the two first are identical in design and possess moreover, as I have tried to prove in the *Secret Doctrine,* seven interpretations varying with their application to either of the three natural kingdoms the physical, the psychic, or the purely spiritual, it will be easily understood that only great initiates are able to correctly interpret the jargon of hermetic philosophers. And then again, since there exist more false than true hermetic writings, even those of Hermes himself may be found distorted. Who does not know for example, that a certain series of formulas may be correctly applied to the solving of concrete problems of technical alchemy while these same on being employed to render an idea belonging to the psychological plane will possess an entirely different meaning? Our late brother Kenneth Mackenzie expresses this well when he says, speaking of Hermetic Societies:

For the practical alchemist whose object was the production of gold by the use of laws belonging especially to his own peculiar art, the evolution of a mystic philosophy was of secondary importance, for his work could be carried on without any direct reference to a system of theosophy, whilst the Sage who had raised himself to a superior plane of metaphysical contemplation rejected naturally the simply material part of his studies, finding it beneath his aspirations.
— *Royal Masonic Cyclopaedia*

Thus it becomes evident that symbols taken as guides to the transmutation of metals, become of small value to those methods which we now call *chemical*. There is yet another question we would like to ask: — Who of our great men would dare to treat as impostors such men as Paracelsus, Van Helmont, Roger Bacon, Boerhaven and many other illustrious alchemists?

While French Academicians mock at the Kabbalah as well as at alchemy (*though at the same time taking from this latter their inspirations and their many discoveries*) the Kabbalists and occultists of Europe begin *sub rosa* to prosecute the Secret sciences of the East. In fact the wisdom of the Orient does not exist for our wise men of the West; it died with the Magi. Nevertheless, alchemy, which if we search diligently we shall find as the foundation of every occult science — comes to them from the far East. Some pretend that it is only the posthumous evolution of the magic of the Chaldeans. We shall try to prove that this latter is only the heir, first to an antediluvian alchemy, and then to an alchemy of the Egyptians. Olaus Borrichius, an authority on this question, tells us to search for its origin in the remotest antiquity.

To what epoch may we ascribe the origin of alchemy? No modern writer is able to tell us exactly. Some give us Adam as its first Adept; others place it to the account of an indiscretion of "the sons of God, who seeing that the daughters of man were beautiful, took them for their wives." Moses and Solomon are later Adepts in the science, for they were preceded by Abraham, who was in turn antedated in the Science of Sciences by Hermes. Is it not Avicenna who says that the Smaragdine Tablet — the oldest existing treatise on Alchemy — was found on the body of Hermes buried centuries ago at Hebron by Sarah the wife of Abraham? But Hermes never was the name of a man, but a generic title, just as in former times we have the Neo-Platonist, and in the present the Theosophist.

What in fact is known about Hermes Trismegistus, or Hermes three times the greatest? Less than we know of Abraham, his wife Sarah and his concubine Agar, which St. Paul declares to be an allegory. Even in the time of Plato, Hermes was already identified with the Thoth of the Egyptians. But this word Thoth does not mean only "intelligence"; it means also "assembly" or school. In truth Thoth Hermes is simply the personification of the *voice* of the priestly caste of Egypt; that is to say of the Grand Hierophants. And if this is

84

the case can we tell at what epoch of prehistoric times this hierarchy of initiated priests began to flourish in the land of Chemi. And even if this were possible we should still be far from having arrived at a complete solution of our problem. For ancient China, no less than ancient Egypt, claims to be the land of the alkahest and of physical and transcendental alchemy; and China may very probably be right. A missionary, an old resident of Pekin, William A. P. Martin, calls it the "cradle of alchemy." Cradle is hardly the right word perhaps, but it is certain that the celestial empire has the right to class herself amongst the very oldest schools of occult Science. In any case alchemy has penetrated into Europe from China as we shall prove.

In the meantime our reader has a choice of solutions, for another pious missionary, Hood, assures us solemnly that alchemy was born in the garden "planted in Haden on the side towards the east." If we may believe him, it is the offspring of Satan who tempted Eve in the shape of a Serpent; but the good man forgot to follow up his assertion to its legitimate conclusion as is proved even by the name of the science. For the Hebrew word for Serpent is Nahash, plural Naha-shim. Now it is from this last syllable *shim* that the words chemistry and alchemy are derived. Is this not clear as day and established in agreement with the severest rules of philology?

Let us now pass to our proofs.

The first authorities in archaic sciences — William Godwin amongst others — have shown us on incontestable evidence that, though alchemy was cultivated by nearly all the nations of antiquity long before our era, the Greeks only began to study it after the beginning of the Christian era and that it only became popularized very much later. Of course by this is meant only the lay Greeks, not of course the Initiates. For the Adepts of the Hellenic temples of Magna Grecia knew it from the days of the Argonauts. The European origin of alchemy dates therefore from this time, as is well illustrated by the allegorical story of the Golden Fleece.

Thus we need only read that which Suidas says in his lexicon with reference to this expedition of Jason, too well known to require telling here:

Deras, the Golden Fleece which Jason and the Argonauts, after a voyage on the Black Sea in Colchis, took with the aid of Medea, daughter of Metes, of Æetes, of Æa. *Only instead of taking that which the poets pretended they took, it was a treatise written on a skin which explained how gold could be made by chemical means.* Contemporaries called this skin of a ram the Golden Fleece, most probably because of the great value attaching to the instructions on it.

This explanation is clearer and much more probable than the erudite vagaries of our modern mythologists, for we must remember that the Colchis of the Greeks is the modern Meretie of the Black Sea; that the Rion, the big river which crosses the country, is the Phasis of the Ancients, which even to this day contains traces of gold; and that the traditions of the indigenous races who live on the shores of the Black Sea, such as the Mingrelians, the Abhaziens and the Meretiens are all full of this old legend of the golden fleece. Their ancestors say they have all been "makers of gold," that is to say they possessed the secret of transmutation which in modern times we call alchemy.

In any case it is certain that the Greeks were ignorant of the hermetic science up to the time of the Neo-Platonists (*towards the end of the fourth and fifth centuries*) with the exception of the initiated, and that they knew nothing of the real alchemy of the ancient Egyptians whose secrets were certainly not revealed to the public at large. In the third century we find the

Emperor Diocletian publishing his famous edict and ordering a careful search to be made in Egypt for books treating of the fabrication of gold, which were collected together and made into a public auto-da-fe. W. Godwin tells us that after this there did not remain one single work on alchemy above ground in the kingdom of the Pharaohs and for the space of two centuries it was never spoken of. He might have added that there remained underground still a large number of such works written on papyrus and buried with the mummies ten times millenarian. The whole secret lies in the power to recognize such a treatise on alchemy in what appears to be only a fairy tale, such as we have in that of the golden fleece or in the romances of the earlier Pharaohs. But it was not the secret wisdom hidden in the allegories of the papyri which introduced alchemy into Europe or the hermetic sciences. History tells us that alchemy was cultivated in China more than sixteen centuries before our era and that it had never been more flourishing than during the first centuries of Christianity. And it is towards the end of the fourth century, when the East opened its ports to the commerce of the Latin races that alchemy once again penetrated into Europe. Byzantium and Alexandria, the two principal centers of this commerce, were quickly inundated with works on the transmutation.

Let us compare the Chinese system with that which is called Hermetic Science.

1. The twofold object which both schools aim at is identical; the making of gold and the rejuvenating and prolonging of human life by means of the *menstruum universale* and *lapis philosophorum*. The third object or true meaning of the "transmutation" has been completely neglected by *Christian* adepts; for being satisfied with their belief in the immortality of the soul, the adherents of the older alchemists have never properly understood this question. Now, partly through

negligence; partly through habit, it has been completely struck out of the *summum bonum* sought for by the alchemists of Christian countries. Nevertheless it is only this last of the three objects which interests the real Oriental alchemists. All initiated adepts despising gold and having a profound indifference for life, cared very little about the first two.

2. Both these schools recognize the existence of two elixirs: the great and the small one. The use of the second on the physical plane transmutes metals and restores youth. The Great Elixir, which was only symbolically an elixir, conferred the greatest boon of all: the immortality of consciousness in the Spirit, the Nirvana which in the sequence of evolution precedes Paranirvana or absolute union with the One Essence.

3. The principles which form the basis of the two systems are also identical, that is to say: the compound nature of metals and their emanation from one common seminal germ. The letter *tsing* in the Chinese alphabet which stands for "germ," and *t'ai*, "matrix," which is found so constantly in Chinese works on alchemy, are the ancestors of the same words which we meet with so frequently in the alchemical treatise of the Hermetists.

4. Mercury and lead, mercury and sulphur are equally in use in the East and in the West, and adding to these many others we find that both schools accepted them under a triple meaning, the last or third of these being that which European alchemists do not understand.

5. The alchemists of both countries accept equally the doctrine of a cycle of transmutation during which the precious metals pass back to their basic elements.

6. Both schools of alchemy are closely allied to astrology and magic.

7. And finally they both make use of a fantastic phraseology, a fact which is noticed by the author of *Studies of Alchemy in China*, who finds that the language of western alchemists, while so entirely different from that of all other western sciences, imitates perfectly the metaphorical jargon of eastern nations, proving that alchemy in Europe had its origin in the far East.

Nor should any prejudices be entertained against alchemy because we say that it is closely connected with astrology and magic. The word magic is an old Persian term which means "knowledge," and embraced the knowledge of all sciences, both physical and metaphysical, studied in those days. The wise and priestly classes of the Chaldeans taught magic, from which came magism and gnosticism. Was not Abraham called a *Chaldean?* And was it not Joseph, a pious Jew, who, speaking of the patriarch, said that he taught mathematics, or the esoteric science, in Egypt, including *the science of the stars,* a professor of magism being necessarily an astrologer?

But it would be a great mistake to confuse the alchemy of the middle ages with that of antediluvian times. As it is understood in the present day it has three principal agents: the philosopher's stone used in the transmutation of metals; the *alkahest* or the universal solvent; and the *elixir vitae* possessing the property of indefinitely prolonging human life. But neither the real philosophers nor the Initiates occupied themselves with the last two. The three alchemical agents, like the Trinity, *one and indivisible,* have become three distinct agents solely through falling under the influence of human egotism. While the sacerdotal caste, grasping and ambitious, anthropomorphized the Spiritual One by dividing it into three persons, the false mystics separated the Divine Force from a universal Kriyasakti and turned it into three agents.

In his *Magie Naturelle* Baptista Porta tells us this clearly: "I do not promise you mountains of gold nor the philosopher's stone, nor even that golden liquor which renders immortal him who drinks it... All that is only visionary; for the world being mutable and subject to change all that it produces must be destroyed."

Geber, the great Arabian alchemist, is even more explicit. He seems, indeed, to have written down the following words with a prophetic forecast of the future: "If we have hidden aught from thee, thou son of science, be not surprised; for we have not hidden it especially from thee, but have made use of a language which will hide the truth from the wicked in order that men who are unjust and ignoble may not understand it. But thou, son of Truth, seek and thou wilt find the gift, the most precious of all. *You, sons of folly, impiety, and profane works, cease endeavoring to penetrate the secrets of this science; for they will destroy you and will hurl you into the most profound misery.*"

Let us see what other writers have to say on the question. Having begun to think that alchemy was after all solely a philosophy entirely metaphysical instead of a physical science (*in which they erred*), they declared that the extraordinary transmutation of base metals into gold was merely a figurative expression for the transformation of man, freeing him of his hereditary evils and of his infirmities in order that he might attain to a degree of regeneration which would elevate him into a divine Being.

This in fact is the synthesis of transcendental alchemy and is its principal object; but this does not for all that represent every end, which this science has in view. Aristotle said in

Alexandria that "the philosopher's stone was not a stone at all, that it is in each man, everywhere, at all times, and is called the final aim of all philosophers."

Aristotle was mistaken in his first proposition though right with regard to the second. On the physical kingdom, the secret of the Alkahest produces an ingredient which is called the philosopher's stone; but for those who care not for perishable gold, the alkahest, as Professor Wilder tells us, is only the *allgeist,* the divine spirit, which dissolves gross matter in order that the unsanctified elements may be destroyed. . . . The *elixir vitae* therefore is only the waters of life which, as Godwin says, "is a universal medicine possessing the power to rejuvenate man and to prolong life indefinitely."

Dr. Kopp, in Germany, published a *History of Chemistry* forty years ago. Speaking of alchemy, looked at especially as the forerunner of modern chemistry, the German doctor makes use of a very significant expression such as the Pythagorean and the Platonist will understand at once. "If," says he, "for the word World we substitute the microcosm represented by man, then it becomes easy to interpret."

Eirenaeus Philalethes declares that:

The philosopher's stone represents the whole universe (or macrocosm) and possesses all the virtues of the great system collected and compressed into the lesser system This last has a magnetic power which draws to it that which affinitises with it in the universe. It is the celestial virtue which spreads throughout creation, but which is epitomized in a miniature abridgment of itself (as man).

Listen to what Alipile says in one of his translated works: "He who knows the microcosm cannot long remain ignorant of the macrocosm. This is why the Egyptians, those zealous investigators of nature, so often said: *Man, know thy Self.*" But their disciples, more restricted in their powers of appreciation, took this adage as being allegorical and in their ignorance inscribed it in their temples. But I declare to you, whoever you may be, who desires to plunge into the depths of Nature, that if that which you seek you do not find within yourself you will never find it without. He who aspires to a first place in the ranks of Nature's students will never find a vaster or better subject of study than he himself presents.

Therefore following in this the example of the Egyptians and in agreement with the Truth which has been shown to me by experience, I repeat these very words of the Egyptians with a loud voice and from the very bottom of my soul, "Oh man, know thyself, for the treasure of treasures is entombed within you."

Eirenaeus Philalethes, cosmopolitan, an English alchemist and Hermetic philosopher, wrote in 1659 alluding to the persecution to which philosophy was subjected:

Many of those who are strangers to the art think that to possess it they must do such and such a thing, like many others we thought so too, but having become more careful and less ambitious of the three rewards (offered by alchemy), on account of the great peril we run we have chosen the only infallible one and the most hidden. . .

And in truth the alchemists were wise so to do. For living in an age when for a slight difference of opinion on religious questions men and women were treated as heretics, placed under a ban and proscribed, and when science was stigmatized as sorcery, then it was quite natural, as Professor A. Wilder says, "that men who cultivate ideas which are out of the general line of thought should invent a symbological language and means of communication amongst themselves which should conceal their identity from those thirsting for their blood."

The author reminds us of the Hindu allegory of Krishna ordering his adopted mother to look into his mouth. She did and saw there the entire universe. This agrees exactly with the Kabbalistic teaching which holds that the microcosm is but the faithful reflection of the macrocosm — a photographic copy to him who understands. This is why Cornelius Agrippa, perhaps the most generally known of all the alchemists, says:

It is a created thing, the object of astonishment both to heaven and earth. It is a compound of the animal, vegetable and mineral kingdoms, it is found everywhere, though recognized by few, and is called by its real name by no one, for it is buried under numbers, signs, and enigmas without the help of which neither alchemy nor natural magic could reach perfection.

The allusion becomes even clearer if we read a certain passage in the *Enchiridion* of Alchemists:

Therefore I will render visible to you in this discourse the natural condition of the philosopher's stone wrapped in its triple garment, this stone of richness and of charity, which holds all secrets and which is a divine mystery the like of which Nature in her sublimity has not in all the world. Observe well what I tell you and remember that it has a triple covering, namely: the Body, the Soul, and the Spirit.

In other words this stone contains the secret of the transmutation of metals, that of the elixir of long life and of *conscious immortality.*

This last secret was the one which the old philosophers chose to unravel, leaving to the lesser lights of modern times the pleasure of wearing themselves out in the attempt to solve the two first. It is the "Word" or the "infallible name," of which

Moses said that there was no need to seek it in distant places "for the Word is close to you; it is in your mouth and in your heart."

Philalethes, the English alchemist, says the same thing in other terms.

Our writings will be like a double-edged knife for the world at large, some will use them to hew out works of art, others will only cut their fingers with them. Nevertheless it is not we who are to blame, since we warn most seriously all those who attempt the task that they are undertaking to master the most elevated philosophy in Nature. And this is so whether we write well or badly. For though we write in English, these writings will be Greek to some who will, nevertheless, persist in believing that they have well understood us, while in reality they distort in the most perverse manner that which we teach; for can it be supposed that those who are naturally fools should become wise simply by reading books which testify to their own natures?

D'Espagnet warned his readers in the same way. He prays the lovers of Nature to read little, and then only those of whom the veracity and intelligence is above suspicion. Let the reader seize quickly a meaning which the author may probably only darkly hint at; for, he adds, truth lives in obscurity; Hermetic philosophers deceive most when they appear to write most clearly, but ever divulge more secrets, the more obscurely they write. The truth cannot be given to the public; even less in these days than in those days when the Apostles were advised not to cast pearls before swine. All these fragments, which we have just cited, are, we hold, so many proofs of that which we have advanced. Outside of the schools of Adepts, almost unapproachable for western students, there does not exist in the whole world — and more especially in Europe, one single work on Occultism, and above all on Alchemy, which is written in clear and precise language, or which offers to the public a system or a method which could be followed as in the physical sciences. All treatises, which come from an Initiate or from an Adept, ancient or modern, unable to reveal all, limit themselves to throwing light on certain problems which are allowed to be disclosed to those worthy of knowing, while remaining at the same time hidden from those who are unworthy of receiving the truth, for fear they should make a selfish use of their knowledge.

Therefore, he, who complaining of the obscurity of writers of the eastern school, should confront them with those of either the middle ages or of modern times which seem to be more clearly written, would prove only two things: first, he deceives his readers in deceiving himself; secondly, he would advertise modern charlatanism, knowing all the time that he is deceiving the public. It is very easy to find semi- modern works which are written with precision and method, but giving only the personal ideas of the writer on the subject, that is to say, of value only to those who know absolutely nothing of the true occult science. We are beginning to make much of Eliphas Levi, who alone knew probably more than all our wise men of the Europe of 1889 put together. But, when once the half-dozen books of the Abbe Louis Constant have been read, re-read and learnt by heart, how far are we advanced in practical Occultism, or even in the understanding of the theories of the Kabbalah? His style is poetical and quite charming. His paradoxes, and nearly every phrase in each of his volumes is one, are thoroughly French in character. But even if we learn them so as to repeat them by heart from the beginning to the end, what pray has he really taught us? Nothing, absolutely nothing — except, perhaps, the French language. We know several of the pupils of this great magician of modern times, English, French and German, all men of learning, of iron wills, and many of whom have sacrificed whole years to these studies. One of his disciples made him a life annuity which he paid him for upwards of ten years, besides paying him 100 francs for every letter when he was obliged to be away. This person at the end of ten years knew less of magic and of the Kabbalah than a chela of ten years standing, of an Indian astrologer.

We have in the library at Adyar his letters on magic in several volumes of manuscripts, written in French and translated into English, and we defy the admirers of Eliphas Levi to show us one single individual who would have become an Occultist even in theory, by following the teaching of the French magician.

Why is this since he evidently got his secrets from an Initiate? Simply because he never *possessed the right to initiate others.* Those who know something of occultism will understand what we mean by this; those who are only pretenders will contradict us, and probably hate us all the more for having told such hard truths.

The secret sciences, or rather the key which alone explains the mystery of the jargon in which they are expressed, cannot be developed; like the Sphinx who dies the moment the enigma of its being is guessed by an Oedipus, they are only occult as long as they remain unknown to the uninitiated. Then again they cannot be bought or sold. A Rosicrucian *"becomes, he is not made"* says an old adage of the Hermetic philosophers, to which the Occultists add, "The science of the gods is mastered by violence; conquered it may be, but it never is to be had for the mere asking." This is exactly what the author of the Acts of the Apostles intended to convey when he wrote the answer of Peter to Simon Magus: "May thy gold perish with thee since thou hast thought that the gifts of God may be bought with money." Occult wisdom should never be used either to make money, or for the attainment of any egotistical ends, or even to minister to personal pride.

Let us go further and say at once that — except in an exceptional case where gold might be the means of saving a whole nation, even the act itself of transmutation when the only motive is the acquisition of riches, becomes black magic. So that neither the secrets of magic nor of occultism, nor of alchemy, can ever be revealed during the existence of our race, which worships the golden calf with an ever increasing frenzy.

Therefore, of what value can those works be which promise to give us the key of initiation for either one or the other of these two sciences, which are in fact only one.

We understand perfectly such Adepts as Paracelsus and Roger Bacon. The first was one of the great harbingers of modern chemistry; the second that of physics. Roger Bacon in his "Treatise on the admirable Forces of Art and of Nature" shows this clearly. We find in it a foreshadowing of all the sciences of our day. He speaks in it of powder for cannons, and predicts the use of steam as a motive power. The hydraulic press, the diving bell, and the kaleidoscope, are all described; he prophesies the invention of flying machines, constructed in such a way that he who is seated in the middle of this mechanical contrivance, in which we easily recognize a type of the modern balloon, has only to turn a mechanism to set in motion artificial wings which begin to beat the air in imitation of those of a bird. Then he defends his brother alchemists against the accusation of using a secret cryptography.

The reason for the secrecy which is maintained by the Wise of all countries is the general contempt and indifference shown for the profounder truths of knowledge, the generality of people being unable to use those things which are of the highest good. Even those amongst them who do have an idea which proves related to something of real utility, owe it generally to chance and their good fortune; so that failing to appreciate its full meaning they fall into scientific errors to the great detriment and ruin, not only of the few, but often of the many.

All of which proves that he who divulges our secrets is worse than foolish, unless he veils that which he discloses to the multitude, and disguises it so cleverly that even the wise understand with difficulty. There are those amongst us who hide their secrets under a certain way of writing, as for example using only consonants so that he who reads this style of writing can only decipher the true meaning when they know the meaning of the words (*the hermetic jargon*). This kind of cryptography was in use amongst the Jews, the Chaldeans, the Syrians, the Arabs, and even the Greeks, and largely adopted in former times especially by the Jews. This is proved by the Hebrew manuscripts of the New Testament, the books of Moses or the Pentateuch rendered ten times more fantastic by the introduction of Masoretic points. But as with the Bible, which has been made to say everything required of it except that which it really did say, thanks to Mesorah and the fathers of the Church, so it was also with Kabbalistic and alchemical books. The key of both having been lost centuries ago in Europe, the Kabbalah (the *good* Kabbalah of the Marquis de Mirville, according to the ex-rabbi, the Chevalier Drach, the pious and most Catholic Hebrew scholar) serves now as a witness confirmatory of both the New and the Old Testaments. According to modern kabbalists, the Zohar is a book of modern prophecies, especially *relating to the Catholic dogmas of the Latin Church,* and is the fundamental stone of the Gospel; which indeed might be true if it were admitted that both in the Gospels and in the Bible, each name is symbolical and each story allegorical; just as was the case with all sacred writings preceding the Christian canon.

Before closing this article, which has already become too long, let us make a rapid *resume* of what we have said.

I do not know if our argument and copious extracts will have any effect on the generality of our readers. But I am sure, at all events, that what we have said will have the same effect on kabbalists and modern *Masters* as the waving of a red rag in front of a bull; but we have long ceased to fear the sharpest horns. These *Masters* owe all their science to the dead letter of the Kabbalah; and to the fantastic interpretation placed on it by some few mystics of the present and the last century, on which "Initiates" of libraries and museums have in their turn made variations, so that they are bound to defend them, tooth and nail. People will see only the raging fire of contest, and he who raises the greatest conflagration will remain the victor. Nevertheless — *Magna est veritas et praevalebit.*

1. It has been asserted that alchemy penetrated into Europe from China, and that falling into profane hands, alchemy (*like astrology*) is no longer the pure and divine science of the schools of Thoth-Hermes of the first Egyptian Dynasties.

2. It is also certain that the Zohar, of which both Europe and other Christian countries possess fragments, is not the same as the Zohar of Simon Ben Yochai, but a compilation of old writings and traditions collected by Moses de Leon of Cordova in the thirteenth century, who, according to Mosheim, has followed in many cases the interpretations which were given him by Christian Gnostics of Chaldea and Syria he went to seek them. The real, old Zohar is only found whole in the Chaldean Book of Numbers, of which there only now exist two or three incomplete copies, which are in the possession of initiated rabbis.

One of these lived in Poland, in strict seclusion, and he destroyed his copy before dying in 1817; as for the other, the wisest rabbi of Palestine, he emigrated from Jaffa some few years ago.

3. Of the real hermetic books there only remains a fragment known as the "Smaragdine Tablet," of which we shall presently speak. All the works compiled on the books of Thoth have been destroyed and burnt in Egypt by the order of Diocletian in the third century of our era. All the others, including Pymander, are in their present form merely recollections, more or less vague and erroneous of different Greek or even Latin authors, who often did not hesitate to palm them off as genuine hermetic fragments. And even if by chance these exist they would be as incomprehensible to the "Masters" of today as the books of the alchemists of the middle ages. In proof of this we have quoted their own thoroughly sincere confessions. We have shown the reasons they give for this (*a*) their mysteries were too sacred to be profaned by the ignorant, being written down and explained only for the use of a few initiates; and they are also too dangerous to be trusted in the hands of those who might mistake their use; (*b*) in the middle ages the precautions taken were ten times as great; for otherwise they stood a good chance of being roasted alive to the great glory of God and His Church.

The key to the jargon of the alchemists and of the real meaning of the symbols and allegories of the Kabbalah only are now to be found in the East. Never having been rediscovered in Europe, what now serves as the guiding star to our modern kabbalists so that they shall recognize the truths in the writings of the alchemists and in the small number of treatises which, written by real initiates, are still to be found in our national libraries?

We conclude, therefore, that in rejecting aid from the only quarter from whence in this our century they may expect to find the Key to the old esotericisms and to the Wisdom religion, they, whether kabbalists, elect of God or modern Prophets, throw to the winds their only chance of studying primitive truths and profiting by them.

At all events we may be assured that it is not the Eastern School which loses by the default.

We have permitted ourselves to say that many French kabbalists have often expressed the opinion that the Eastern school could never be worth much, no matter how it may pride itself on possessing secrets unknown to Europeans *because it admits women into its ranks.*

To this we might answer by repeating the fable told by brother Jos. N. Nutt, Grand Master of the Masonic lodges of the United States for women, to show what women would do if they were not shackled by males — whether as men or as god.

A lion passing close by a monument representing an athletic and powerful figure of a man tearing the jaws of a lion said: "If the scene which this represents had been executed by a lion the two figures would have changed places." The same remark holds good for Woman. If only she were allowed to represent the phases of human life she would distribute the parts in reverse order. She it was who first took Man to the Tree of Knowledge, and made him know Good and Evil; and if she had been let alone and allowed to do that which she wished, she would have led him to the Tree of Life and thus rendered him immortal.

Psychic and Spiritual Development

by Annie Besant

To speak properly, the title of my lecture should be Psychic Development and Spiritual Unfolding. That would have made rather too long a title, and yet the difference between the words development and unfolding is a very important one. When we are dealing with the Spirit we cannot accurately speak of development. A Spirit neither develops nor evolves; he only unfolds into manifestation that which eternally lies within him. A Spirit, being identical with the Universal Consciousness, can neither increase nor diminish. What he can do, entering into conditions of time and space, is to turn outwards that which is within, to turn attention outwards, and slowly to conquer, by this contact with matter, that knowledge of the universe regarded as phenomenal, which does not come into his consciousness when he is separated off from the universal by that delicate film of matter which is his vehicle in the nirvanic, or spiritual, sphere. Within that seed of Divinity all possibilities are contained. It is only the turning outwards which is possible, by the contact with the various planes of matter.

On the other hand, with regard to psychic development, which depends entirely on the conditions of the matter which veils the Spirit, the word development is entirely accurate. Psychic progress is literally the evolving and developing of form after form, the forms being separate the one from the other, and being, as regards three of them, new-born at each birth, and dying one after the other in the process of death and of after-death. So that we are face to face with two entirely different processes, which I propose to try to make rather more clear than they are in the minds of many.

These two things are fundamentally different in nature. They belong to those two great opposites by the interaction of which the universe is built — Spirit, Matter, You cannot have two things more absolutely opposed. You may reach that which is Spirit by denying one after the other all the qualities and manifestations of matter. There ought, then, to be a very wide gulf in the minds of students with regard to that which belongs to the development of the psychic, and that which belongs to the unfolding of the Spirit, and if we can get rid of the confusion that exists so largely amongst us we shall not have wasted time.

Let us glance first at the spiritual and ask what it is. Carry your mind to the higher or spiritual Triad, that reproduction of the Monad as Spirit in his threefold nature, as Will, Intuition and Intellect, sometimes called Âtma-buddhi-manas. The Monad himself is the essence and root of Spirit, the Spirit being his reproduction in the three higher spheres of our fivefold system, showing out his three aspects of Power, Wisdom and Activity; these are manifested by the ray of the Monad appropriating an atom from each of the three spheres, the spiritual, intuitional and intellectual; these condition the manifestation of the monad, each variety of matter showing forth one aspect only, as though the three aspects were separable. Not one of these really exists in separation; where Spirit shows himself forth as Will in the spiritual sphere, there are also present, though subordinate, the two aspects of the Monad which appear in the two succeeding spheres, Intuition and Intellect; both are present in that âtmic particle, and form part of its consciousness, although dominated by that Will by which Âtma shows himself forth. So again when you take the second aspect, showing itself forth as Intuition (Buddhi), you

104

cannot separate off from that either Will (Âtma) or Intellect (Manas); they are both implicitly present, although it is the Wisdom aspect of the Monad which is there dominant. And so with the third. When we come to intellect, showing forth the active, or creative aspect of the Monad, there also we have to recognize the implicit presence of Will and Intuition. Consciousness is one, and it can never show out one aspect alone without the other two being present, You will find it is laid down by one of the greatest of Indian psychologists that we have here continually a reflection and a re-reflection within the Self and that when we speak of one of them we are thinking of that aspect as working upon itself, and so showing forth that quality predominantly; but that in that same sphere we have the other two aspects, colored indeed, as it were, by the first; in each case all three are present, two as reflected on to the third, that third dominating the two reflections. And in this way is made up a ninefold division, giving a marvelously accurate classification. But for us just now it is enough to recognize one dominant aspect and two others implicitly present.

When we come down from those two and a half higher spheres, where the true spiritual Triad shows itself forth, to the lower two and a half spheres we come into the world where matter is dominant. In the higher, consciousness prevails, over matter. In the lower, matter prevails over consciousness. The division of higher and lower comes in the middle of the mental sphere, so that the three sub-planes belong to the world of Spirit predominantly, the lower four belonging predominantly to the world of phenomena. In the lower spheres the matter which there enveils the Spirit conditions it far more forcibly and obviously than does the matter on the higher; and the work of the Spirit on those lower planes will be the moulding and organizing of matter, in the effort to create for himself vehicles which will express him in the lower world, and deprive him as little as possible of his own inherent powers.

In that lower world also you will see this same triplicity of manifestation continually showing forth, though there again one aspect predominates over the others. For instance, in the emotional sphere, the astral body serves for the vehicle of activity and thought as well as for the vehicle of emotion, and the man working in the astral sphere is the same man as the man working here, with none of his consciousness lost, and showing out the three faces, as they also show out here in the physical body. There is always a danger, as we analyze man into factors, of losing sight of this unit nature of consciousness. When we are dealing with the physical body we recognize the aspects of consciousness and their places of manifestation; we understand quite well that the mental aspect works through the cerebro-spinal nerves, the emotional through the sympathetic system and glands, the volitional through the muscles; all are present. We must do the same with the astral and mental spheres. This close study of consciousness and its vehicles is absolutely necessary for a real understanding of Spirituality and Psychism.

When we study the spiritual, we are dealing with consciousness in the higher spheres, the characteristic mark of which is unity. He, says Shrl Krishna, "who seeth Me in all things, and all things in Me, he seeth, verily he seeth". Nothing other than that is spiritual vision. There is no vision entitled to be called spiritual, save that which sees God in Nature and Nature in God, which recognizes the One Universal Bliss, the One Universal Self-Consciousness, the One Universal Existence, and sees all things rooted in THAT and in THAT alone. To realize the Self-Consciousness is alone Wisdom. And we must bear clearly in mind this definition of the Spirit, that it is the consciousness of Unity, of Oneness with the Supreme. Again it is written: "There is nothing moving or unmoving that can exist bereft of Me". That is everywhere to be seen and,

106

recognized, and none may call himself spiritual if he does not to some extent enjoy that realization of the Oneness. Spirituality is an exceedingly different thing from Psychism, which is the manifestation of Intellect, cognizing the external worlds, and seeing the differences, the diversity, in all those worlds. It does not matter whether you are looking at physical, astral, or mental objects; all looking at objects, all the activity of consciousness utilizing matter as a means of contact with objects, is covered by the word Psychism. It depends for its development on the organization of the sheaths, on their delicacy and refinement; and for the purpose of understanding this, it is enough to think of the human being as composed of consciousness and matter, taking the three lower sheaths simply as the sense-garment. Drop for a moment the thought of the physical, astral, and mental bodies the word body seems to connote too much of difference; they are only matter at different stages of density, and the three together make up the sense-garment of the consciousness, Throughout the psychic development, the improvement of the sense-garment is the task which the student has before him; He wants to make each layer of the sense-garment more refined, more sensitive, and to realize it more and more clearly as a garment and not as himself — one garment in three layers. All the evolution that goes on in that garment improves psychic development, bringing the mind into fuller touch with the external world. If that be clearly grasped, you cannot confuse the psychic and the spiritual, for one belongs wholly to the consciousness in its unity, and the other to the sense-garment in its multiplicity. And you will be inclined neither to overvalue nor to undervalue psychic development. Students are inclined to run into extremes. Neither extreme position is true. One should take the common-sense view of what is called psychism. Psychism is the manifestation of consciousness through its sense-garment, and everything that increases the translucency of that garment, in one or other of these layers, is part of psychic development. In our present stage of evolution a large part of this psychic development is going on in the astral body. Consciousness has largely conquered the physical layer of the sense-garment in most people, and is beginning to conquer the astral layer; but as that progress is at present abnormal, it is regarded as something almost supernatural, instead of being taken in the same quiet common-sense way that you take the higher orders of the physical senses amongst ourselves. We know the good musician has a much more delicate ear than most of us, but we do not look on him as apart from us because of that. Taking that delicacy a little further and carrying it to the next layer of the sense-garment does not alter its quality. It is a question of degree and not of kind. In the physical part of the garment, the lowest layer of the body, there is a sharper division between the senses than there is in other layers. In the mental sphere the consciousness which has not yet touched the physical has a keen recognition of the life within an object, and a very confused impression of the garment of matter in which that consciousness is veiled, the garment which makes it an object. So also, coming down into the emotional, or astral sphere, if you take a consciousness that has had no experience of the physical plane at all (as in the Elemental Kingdom) you will find that the entities do not receive from the astral object the clearly defined outline, but a far more blended impression. There are no sharp lines of distinction between the senses; hearing and sight, for instance, melt into one another. It is true that you can point to one part and say: that is sight, and to another: that is hearing, but you come to a place where you cannot distinguish clearly between the two senses, for that clear definition takes place for the first time on the physical plane. Only consciousness, having once obtained that definition, does not lose it when it is active in the second layer of the sense-garment. It keeps the definition, and that is what is gained from the physical body, even when the physical body is finally thrown off. Consciousness having passed through the physical sphere

108

never again loses that clearness and definiteness which in the physical sphere it gained. So that when you come to the psychic evolution in the second layer, the astral, you find the advantage of the consciousness having passed through the physical stage.

There is another phrase that comes into my mind from the great Scripture I have already quoted: without senses enjoying sense objects — a phrase which sounds extremely strange and rather unintelligible. The reason is the one I have just spoken of, that the clear definition of the powers of perception in the consciousness is not dependent on the organs, after the organs have served their purpose and have given to it the necessary definition. It is said even of the LOGOS Himself, who is spoken of in that verse; having passed through all these experiences, He has carried with Him to that lofty rank of Divinity the qualities which in the humbler days of earth, in far-off universes, He slowly gathered and built into Himself as we are building them now.

The whole of the development of consciousness in the sense-garment is psychic, whether in one layer or another. You should not limit the word to the astral and mental spheres, for by making a difference of term in that way you lose the sense of the unity of evolution.

The evolution of the astral body largely takes place from the mental sphere, as the organization of the physical senses and their apparatus takes place from the astral sphere. As you are working in the developing of your mind now, that mind, in its more evolved stage, fashions for itself that astral layer of the sense-garment which it will be able to use more independently as evolution proceeds. And to develop healthily that second layer, it must be developed from above and not from below. It is possible to stimulate the growth of the sense-organs in the astral body to some extent from the physical senses, but such stimulation does not carry us very far. Also, it has the tendency to injure the physical organs used, and what is more serious, to injure in the brain those particular centers which, in the later evolution of the astral senses, would be their proper points of expression on the physical plane. For within our brain are certain centers which are the places of junction between the astral and physical sense-organs, making possible the bringing down of the information gathered by the astral into the physical consciousness working through the brain. Suppose the astral chakra; which answers to astral sight, is active. That has its corresponding point between the eye-brows, and a certain development of a center in the physical body between the eyebrows goes on as the result of the development of that astral sense in the astral body. It is that which lies at the root of the practice of some people in psychometry, and a little-developed form of clairvoyance, where they sometimes put an object to the forehead when trying to psychometrise, or to see with the astral sight. That particular center and the solar plexus are the two chief centers in making a link of connection between the astral and physical layers of the sense-garment. But if, instead of stimulating from the physical, you stimulate from the mental, then your astral centers develop healthily and naturally, and with that will come, without any very special effort, the descent of the information gathered in that second layer into the first, so that you become consciously clairvoyant, clairaudient, and so on.

When those faculties appear in the waking consciousness the person is called a psychic or a sensitive; and the name means nothing more than this: that there is a beginning of the shaping of those senses, and that the links between the two layers of the sense-garment are beginning to work. It is a great advantage for the gaining of knowledge to have the astral senses as well as the physical at your disposal; but it will only give you more phenomenal knowledge; it will

110

not quicken your spiritual unfolding. Nay, it may possibly delay it, because it makes the phenomenal more attractive than before. It is more difficult for the person in whom these finer senses are developed to turn away from the outer and more attractive phenomena, and to fix the attention inwards to evoke the true spiritual vision, the knowledge of the One.

It is for that reason that in many of the ancient books — whether Indian, Grecian, or Egyptian — you find so little stress laid on the development of these higher sensuous powers. It is seen that sometimes the person in whom they are developed is thereby made more separate and not more united; whereas in the spiritual unfolding, the spiritual person feels himself more one with every form of life and less separate. In India the siddhis are definitely regarded as having no part in spiritual development, and those who try to develop them are simply looked at in the same light as those who try to develop keener physical sight or hearing.

The training for psychic development and for spiritual unfoldment is quite different. In psychic development you have to deal with the perfection and organisation of the sense-garment; when you come to deal with the spiritual, the preparation is intellectual, emotional, and moral. I do not mean, in saying that, that morality as such, or the lower intelligence as such, is spiritual; but they are the necessary preparation for the manifestation of the Spirit in man. The growth of the moral character, of self-sacrifice, self-surrender, willingness to serve, the breaking away — of the sense of separateness — all this is the preparation for spiritual unfolding. And so also with regard to the higher intelligence. It is absolutely necessary for the spiritual manifestation; and everything that tends to purify the intelligence and raise it from the concrete to the abstract is an approach towards the region where the spiritual unfolding will take place. Hence the immense stress laid in all ancient books on the building up of virtue on the one side, and of intelligence on the other; so that within the good man and the reasonable man, the spiritual man might descend and find his habitation. Truly, as it is said in Light on the Path, "great though the gulf may be between the good man and the sinner . . . it is immeasurable between the good man and the one on the threshold of Divinity". That is true. It is a difference in kind and not only in degree. Hence it is that when you are striving to quicken the evolution of man, so that the Spirit may reveal himself within the garb of matter, so much stress is laid on study and on moral training, not as confusing the two, but the one as being the pathway which makes it possible for the other to manifest. The Spirit cannot manifest in the ignorant or in the immoral man; he is latent within him, and until that preparation is made, spiritual unfoldment and manifestation in the world of forms cannot be. I know that that puts spiritual unfolding very high, and it may shock some people, because whatever is vague they think is spiritual. But really that is not so. A good emotion does not mean consciousness on the buddhic plane. Emotion is not spirituality, although it is often confused with it. There is an enormous gulf between them. Spirituality is the Self-consciousness, conqueror over matter, not the manifestation distorted and stunted in matter, which is emotion. That truth to some people may seem rather cold. It is, of course, nothing of the kind. It is the most inspiring truth which it is possible to put forward, when a glimpse is caught of what it really means; for there is nothing discouraging in recognising that we have a long path to travel before reaching the spiritual heights. It would be far more discouraging if the small manifestations of emotion and good feeling we find down here were the limit of the Divine in humanity. That they are very often beautiful, I do not deny; but they are not the Beauty: that is something wider, vaster, grander, than you or I at present can even conceive. Surely it is more inspiring to the heart and mind to see far off the dawn of a grandeur that some day we know will be ours, than it is to rest content with the miserable and petty manifestations which are all we are capable of at the present time. The one inspires to ceaseless effort, to unwearied aspiration; the other makes us sit down contentedly, thinking we are almost near the manifestation of God in ourselves. But, as we catch a glimpse of those greater possibilities, as we put our thought of Spirit higher and higher, we become more conscious of a strength within ourselves which makes us mighty enough to rise above the highest that we can dream. Only we need time and patience, a high ideal, and noble thinking. One thing only is the sign that the Spirit in us is beginning to put forth his powers; the possession of peace, serenity, strength, and broadness of view. Those show the germinating of the divine seed within us; and as we see those qualities grow we cannot say: "I am spiritually developed," but we may dare to say: " My face is turned in the right direction, and I am beginning to tread the Path which leads to the manifestation of the Spirit."

The Scorpions of Isis

by M. A. Murray

I am Isis, the great Goddess, the Mistress of Magic, the Speaker of Spells.

I came out of my house which my brother Set had given to me, for Thoth called to me to come, Thoth the twice great, mighty of truth in earth and in heaven. He called, and I came forth when Ra descended in glory to the western horizon of heaven, and it was evening.

And with me came the seven scorpions, and their names were Tefen and Befen, Mestet and Mestetef, Petet, Thetet, and Matet. Behind me were Tefen and Befen; on either side were Mestet and Mestetef; in front were Petet, Thetet, and Matet, clearing the way that none should oppose or hinder me. I called aloud to the scorpions, and my words rang through the air and entered into their ears, "Beware of the Black One, call not the Red One, look neither at children nor at any small helpless creature."

Then I wandered through the Land of Egypt, Tefen and Befen behind me, Mestet and Mestetef on either side of me, Petet, Thetet, and Matet before me; and we came to Per-sui, where the crocodile is God, and to the Town of the Two Sandals, which is the city of the Twin Goddesses. Here it is that the swamps and marshes of the North Country begin, where there are fields of papyrus-reeds, and where the marshmen dwell; from here to the Great Green Waters is the North Land.

Then we came near houses where the marsh-people dwelt, and the name of one of the women was "Glory," though some called her "Strength" also. She stood at her door, and from afar she saw me coming, wayworn and weary, and I would fain have sat me down in her house to rest. But when I would have spoken to her, she shut the door in my face, for she feared the seven scorpions that were with me.

I went farther, and one of the marshwomen opened her door to me, and in her house I rested. But Mestet and Mestetef, Petet, Thetet, and Matet, and Befen also, they came together and laid their poison upon the sting of Tefen; thus, the sting of Tefen had sevenfold power. Then returned Tefen to the house of the woman Glory, she who had closed her door against me; the door was still shut, but between it and the threshold was a narrow space. Through this narrow space crept Tefen and entered the house, and stung with a sting of sevenfold power the son of the woman Glory. So fierce and burning was the poison that the child died and fire broke out in the house.

Then the woman Glory cried and lamented, but no man hearkened to her, and Heaven itself sent water upon her house. A great marvel was this water from Heaven, for the time of the inundation was not yet.

Thus, she mourned and lamented, and her heart was full of sorrow when she remembered how she had shut her door in my face when, weary and wayworn, I would have rested in her house. And the sound of her grief came to my ears, and my heart swelled with sorrow for her sorrow, and I turned back and went with her to where her dead child lay.

And I, Isis, the Mistress of magic, whose voice can awake the dead, I called aloud the Words of Power, the Words that even the dead can hear. And I laid my arms upon the child

116

that I might bring back Life to the lifeless. Cold and still he lay, for the sevenfold poison of Tefen was in him. Then did I speak magical spells to the poison of the scorpions, saying, "O poison of Tefen, come out of him and fall upon the ground! Poison of Befen, advance not, penetrate no farther, come out of him, and fall upon the ground! For I am Isis, the great Enchantress, the Speaker of spells. Fall down, O poison of Mestet! Hasten not, poison of Mestetef! Rise not, poison of Petet and Thetet! Approach not, poison of Matet! For I am Isis, the great Enchantress, the Speaker of spells. The child shall live, the poison shall die! As Horus is strong and well for me, his mother, so shall this child be strong and well for his mother!"

Then the child recovered, and the fire was quenched, and the rain from heaven ceased. And the woman Glory brought all her wealth, her bracelets and her neck-ornaments, her gold-work and silver-work, to the house of the marshwoman, and laid them at my feet in token of repentance that she had shut the door upon me when, weary and wayworn, I had come to her house.

And to this day men make dough of wheat-flour kneaded with salt and lay it upon the wound made by the sting of a scorpion, and over it they recite the Words of Power which I recited over the child of the woman Glory when the sevenfold poison was in him. For I am Isis, the great Enchantress, the Mistress of magic, the Speaker of spells.

The Astral Light

by Louise A. Off

The Astral Light, as the source of all world phenomena, is a theme of no little importance to the student of occultism.

The root of the word "Astral" is to be found in the Assyrian *Istar,* signifying star, and was applied to this element by the Kabalists and later mystics, because they considered the heavenly bodies as the concrete crystallizations of the Astral Light. Some Theosophic writers have confounded the nature of this element with that of Akasâ, while in fact the latter comprehends infinitely more both in quality and quantity. Literally the Sanskrit term Akasâ means the sky, but occultly the *impalpable* Ether or the Soul within the Ether. Our most logical authority, *The Secret Doctrine,* defines it as the "immortal spirit," the progenitor of Cosmic life and "universal intelligence whose *characteristic property* is Buddhi." Akasâ is the sphere of the pure undifferentiated *Monad,* the essence of wisdom, while the Astral Light at its opposite pole is the abstract atom of matter, the plane of generation, and the great womb out of which issues all planetary life. Ether, which is the highest vibration of the Astral Light, is but as a vehicle for Akasâ, a gross body in comparison.

The functions of the Astral Light are as manifold as the expressed universe. Its nature is dual — the highest Ether forming its positive, and the concrete, or differentiated elements, its negative pole. Its cause reaches back to the root of all causes, and its effects involve all our physical and psychical experiences. We deal with its familiar phenomena in every breath and every motion, while the rare and abnormal

119

phases are as strictly subject to its laws. It is not substantially identical with any one of the material elements of Cosmic matter, but is one degree superior to *Prakriti* (Nature as apprehended by the senses), and it impenetrates and vitalizes each atom. It is itself the one underlying element in which all other known elements have their source and supply. In its physical aspects it includes the Ether of modern scientists, but in the metaphysical sense they scarcely touch its borderland. For while it is the reservoir of Heat, Light, Magnetism, and Electricity — the field of all degrees of vibration — it is also the sphere of all intellectual life, and the ruling agent in the alchemical process which frees the cerebral atom and converts it into thought. Its vibratory rate determines individual mental tendencies, and also establishes our intimate relations in body with the stars. Paracelsus maintains that, "as fire passes through an iron stove, so do the stars pass through man with all their properties, and go into him as the rain into the earth, which gives fruit out of that same rain." While the modern spectroscope reveals the identity in substance of infinitesimal man, and the greatest luminiferous body that glides in vast revolutions through space, no instrument has, as yet, been discovered so sensitive as to register the subtle and evanescent fluid which, by its uniform nature, makes astronomical research and thought- transference possible. Keely's motor has, however, already foreshadowed such a discovery.

The Astral Light is the great record-book upon whose pages every thought and act of differentiated consciousness is engraven, there to be read by the individual who has learnt the secret of exalting his vibrations until they become synchronous with the waves of this finer element. The definition of Memory which has ever been the enigma of science, a function with an inapprehensible cause, is related to the domain of the occultist, who may briefly define it as the correlative vibration of the cerebral center with the Astral Light. Within this correlation reside all the possibilities of consciousness from the horizon of Maya (Illusion) to the zenith of pure Ether or transcendental life. Madame Blavatsky sweepingly states: "The Psychic forces, the 'ideomotor' and 'electro-biological powers', 'latent thought' and even 'unconscious cerebration' theories can be condensed into two words, the Kabalistic 'Astral Light'." Quesne treated of it as a universally diffused fluid permeating all things, and differing in action only according to the mobility of the organism by which it is confined.

The differentiated *will to live* accompanying each primary monad is the sculptor of the astral images which constitute individual experience. An intense power of concentration makes these images subjective, in which case they are realities only to the operator, but under still more acute and intelligent development, these images may assume a concrete objective form with power of duration proportioned to the original impulse or determined purpose of the projector. "Determined will," says a fire-philosopher, "is a beginning of all magical operations," and the great magician, Abbé Constant, states; "To acquire magical power, two things are necessary: to disengage the will from all servitude and to exercise it in control." He alone can become a master whose physical and psychical organization is attuned to the Astral Keynote — whose self-consciousness has outgrown the limits of personal slavery, and whose will is so cultivated as to act without fear and without desire — intelligent, determined, self-possessed and confident. While the majority of mankind is occupied in mere negative registration of sense-impressions the occultist classifies these, and admits only those most useful to his purpose. Colonel Olcott refers to the manipulation of the Astral Light in his statement, that "the efficacy of all words used as charms and spells lies in what the Indian Aryas call the *vach,* a certain latent power resident in Akasa. Physically we may describe it as the power to set up certain measured vibrations, not in the grosser atmospheric particles whose undulations beget light, sound, heat and electricity, but in the latent spiritual principle or force — about the nature of which modern science knows almost nothing." As an illustration of this we have the word *Aum,* which, as all students know, has an equilibrating effect which resists the inroad of passion.

The symbol used to express the astral realm by the mystics of all ages is the serpent, or the "fiery dragon." It is stated that long before our globe or even our universe became egg-shaped, "a long trail of Cosmic dust (or fire mist) moved and writhed like a serpent in space." This was the beginning of our Eternity, exoterically expressed by a serpent with its tail in its mouth, or in the act of incubating the *Mundane Egg* with its fiery breath. The Chaldean Oracles refer to the Astral Light as "winding in form," which qualification refers to the vibratory motion that characterizes it. The intense rate of its pulsation may be faintly realized in the rapidity with which successive images are recorded in the dreaming or hypnotized state. An illustration is recounted of a student who was making scientific experiments in this psychological field with a friend. While a drop of water was descending down upon his forehead, he closed his eyes and dreamed that he started out from a harbor upon the wide main, soon passing several beautiful islands full of villages, cities, verdant fields and mountains. The sun was beaming generously, but little by little the sky grew darker and heavier, and drifts of black clouds swept upon the scene. A great gale arose. Consternation and horror pervaded the crew. The waves began to rise higher and higher, until finally the heavens and the sea were blended into one dense chaos. The crisis was at hand. The dreamer suddenly felt as though the whole sea had burst asunder and drawn him in — he awoke just as the drop of water touched his skin, fallen from the hand of his friend and held but a few inches above his head. He had registered the full episode of dramatic changes during the instant in which the sensor nerve flashed its irritation to the brain. Far more remarkable than this are illustrations on record which cover an extent of years and are recorded in an instant of time, experimentally proven to be less than the period required for transmitting a nervous current. The wondrous rapidity with which feeling and thinking may be condensed has also been frequently analyzed in the experience of persons nearly drowned, and as Helmholtz has demonstrated that the period in which a nerve-current may be conducted is a *definite* one, we have no alternative but to assume that a far subtler element or vehicle is employed in registering psychic experiences. By the astral current throughout the auras, around the nerve-centers and nerve-tubes, mind contracts mind, thoughts are flashed in upon us and emotions conveyed. It radiates from the individual man as an impalpable but intelligent aura - the medium of his psychic and intuitional life, by means of which he evinces sympathy and understanding; while in its higher aspect it is the sensitive plane that records Cosmic ideation, and conveys impressions of truth and of universal law to the human mind.

Experiments with trained sensitives has proven that when an intellectual concept is formed, the astral aura photographs it instantaneously, while, when an emotion is evinced, the aura changes in intensity of color, and, on volition becoming manifest, there is a positive increase of vibration. We, therefore, carry with us all we have ever thought and felt — and *self* is the ever-refining essence of this thought and feeling. From this point of view responsibility assumes enormous proportions, and we perceive why the great Teachers of the world have ever agreed that Man is his own heaven and his own hell.

The great mesmerizer, Du Potet, declares that the faculty of directing this fluid is inherent in certain organizations, that it passes through all bodies, and that everything can be used as a conductor — *"no chemical or physical forces are able to destroy it."* Treating thus with the merest initial of this latent power, who can say where its further unfoldment will lead the collective consciousness of Humanity?

In the present age, our science informs us, we perceive in the main only the lowest vibrations and inferior qualities of the Astral Light, because we are in the lower arc of our present cycle, and the energy of the life-wave is at its ebb. Mme. Blavatsky says of Plato's method of expression that he "divides the intellectual progress of the universe during every cycle into fertile and barren periods..... When those circulations, which Eliphas Levi calls 'currents of the Astral Light' in the universal Ether, ...take place in harmony with the divine spirit, our earth and everything pertaining to it enjoys a fertile period. The occult powers of plants, animals, and minerals magically sympathize with its superior natures, and the divine soul of man is in perfect intelligence with these inferior ones. But during the barren periods the latter lose all their magic sympathy, and the spiritual sight of the majority of mankind is so blinded as to lose every notion of the superior power of its own divine spirit. We are in a barren period." Ignoring our latent inherent forces, we drift in negative submission to the lower laws of Nature, suffer deprivation, want of thought, emotion, and volition, while the precious fluid, in mute anticipation, haunts our dreamless sleep, and awaits the dawning of a higher Consciousness.

Aspects of the Christ

by Annie Besant

I have chosen for our thought tonight a subject which appears to me to be one of profound interest, and one also of great practical importance. For no subject in the western world touches more nearly the hearts of men than the subject of the Christ. Round that name are entwined all sacred memories, all loftiest aspirations, the ideal of a perfect manhood, the manifestation of God Himself. On the other hand there are many intellectual questions concerned with it, and it is impossible to escape from those questions in the modern world of historical discussions as to the date at which He lived; critical discussions as to the authenticity of the records in which His life is inscribed; dogmatic controversies as to His nature, whether He be God and man, God or man, or only man; whether His rightful place is that of a great Teacher or of a supreme Object of worship; how He lived and how he died; all these are questions which grow up around His name; these are questions that the intellect must decide.

Now when you come to the atmosphere of the intellect, you inevitably come into that which is and must be critical, calm, balanced, more or less cold. Whereas on the other side the deepest, the most passionate emotions of human nature are concerned - emotions of reverence to God, emotions of passionate admiration of man, emotions of aspiration towards the spiritual life, aspirations the holiest and the deepest. And hence we find that round the intellectual discussions have raged the floods of emotional feelings, to the injury of both. Everywhere the emotions come in, the intellect becomes biased and cannot judge aright. Where the intellect is concerned emotions are a danger, not a help. But on the other hand the emotions concerned being those which are the most inspiring, the most elevating, the most spiritualizing, it is necessary that they should have their place, that they should enjoy full liberty of expression, that they should go out to the Object of worship, that they should purify the heart as well as inspire the life. We cannot do either without the intellect or without the emotions. Both have their place, both have their value; but in order that each may have its full value it must have its rightful place assigned to it in this great central subject of religious thought. The intellect must be given its full, free play, the emotions their undisturbed expansion. And we shall only be able, I think, effectively to do that if we regard the whole subject in that light of the Divine Wisdom which includes the intellect and the emotions, but which also recognizes the place and the supremacy of the Spirit. And I want if I can tonight to help you to a view which it seems to me - if it commends itself to you, and if you study it - may help you to understand, as you should understand by the intellect, but may leave to you untouched, nay, untouchable and invulnerable, that Christ of the human heart to whom the Spirit raises himself in his moments of highest realization, far away from every wind of controversy, from every storm of discussion, in that pure unclouded air of the very heaven itself, where intuition sees and reason bows down in silence, where, the Spirit speaks and all lesser voices are dumb.

Let us take first the intellectual view and glance at this historically, of the life itself, and then, from the standpoint, still intellectual, of comparative religion. Let us then glance at the dogmatic side, round which so much of controversy has raged and still may rage. Then let us see how the Christ appears as the Ideal of the soul, and how He rises above all the controversies of history and of doctrine in that mighty, all- compelling form which has been called the "Logos of the soul". If thus perchance we can study some of the many aspects we may be able to keep the inspiration of the ideal untouched, and may walk calmly, thoughtfully, in study careful and accurate, amid all the intellectual difficulties that have surrounded the subject in the past, that inevitably still surround it today. And let me say, ere beginning this intellectual part of our study, that if there is one subject more than another which should be a subject to unite and not to divide, it is that of the thought of the Lord of Love, of Him who is to be the Buddha of Love, as the Lord Gautama was the Buddha of Wisdom. Round that sacred name the battles of the churches long have raged. The name which should unite according to the prayer " that they all may be one, as I, Father, am in Thee, that they also may be one in us," that prayer has fallen, as it were, unregarded to the earth, has brought down no answer, has found no acceptance; for Christians have quarreled over Christ more bitterly than perhaps over anything else. And sad indeed and terrible would it be if we, who preach the brotherhood of religions, should copy that worst side which makes the holiest subjects, subjects of controversy, and raises the storm of human passion within what should be the Holy of Holies of the Sanctuary.

To avoid this let us look at the intellectual side quietly and calmly as befits students. First the historical. On that Occultism speaks clearly and distinctly, as we have learned from the Masters of the White Lodge, from the messenger whom They sent to us, Madame Blavatsky, confirmed by the study of later workers. And this view is supported by much in the story of the past and by one or two teachings that are worthy of consideration in the record of the New Testament itself. It is the story of a Hebrew youth, born about a century before the beginning of the Christian era, trained partly in Egypt, partly in the monasteries of the Essenes, coming forth at about the age of thirty to be a teacher among his people, recognized by them as known in the days of his youth. On him

127

descended the Spirit of the Holiest, and, descending, on him it abode, and in that moment of descent was the coming of the Christ to occupy the chosen body which lie had selected for His stay on earth. Then a brief life of three years among men, a life of uttermost beneficence, a life of many wondrous healings as well as of exquisite teaching. The gathering together round Him of a few to whom He taught the deeper doctrines some of which they later were to spread abroad; "Unto you it is given to know the mysteries of the kingdom of God, but to others in parables." Sometimes the enthusiastic love of the crowd, sometimes the passionate hatred, attempting life; finally in the city of Jerusalem, in the very court of the Temple itself, a riot breaking out, a terrible stoning, the passing back of the Christ to His own place, the murder of the body in which He had dwelt, the taking up of the body, the hanging of it in mockery on a tree by those who had slain Him. Such is the ancient story, the story of the records of the past, confirmed by traditions which have passed downward through the Hebrew people, who tell us of this young Teacher in the days of Queen Salome, who preached and taught, who was slain and hanged on a tree. And it is confirmed by those words spoken by S. Peter, recorded in the Acts of the Apostles, when, speaking reproachfully to the Hebrews of his day, he spoke of "Jesus whom ye slew and hanged upon a tree". Then, still following the record, how the Christ for forty years and more continued to come to His disciples, teaching, guiding, instructing, inspiring them for the great work that was to be done; how gradually they dispersed over the nations, gathering disciples and carrying on the work, until in the later days that great recruit was won to whom the Christ Himself appeared sending him forth on his great mission, he who laid the foundations of the Church as Church, the great Apostle Paul, who declared that he knew naught among them save Christ Jesus and Him crucified. And then the spread as known to you, the spread of the doctrines of the great Teacher; and side by side with the

128

outer preaching, the Mysteries of Jesus. The teachings in those, as I said, were begun by the Christ Himself and carried on for some forty years or more. Forty years is the time given by one of the great Bishops of the early Church. We should be inclined to make it somewhat longer than that, but the date has not been very carefully measured. Then the birth of Apollonius of Tyana, he who was sometimes called the Pagan Christ, the disciple Jesus reborn in the year 1 of the Christian era, taking up the work, travelling far and wide, Messenger of the great White Lodge, making in various places in Europe centers of occult force to be used long, long afterwards when again a great Teacher should appear, passing away out of the body and taking up the work of the Mysteries of Jesus, becoming the great Teacher of the Mysteries, instructing, guiding, helping during the following centuries. One writer among the early Fathers of those Mysteries, one great Bishop who underwent martyrdom, tells us how he was taught in the Mysteries, and how the angels came to teach; gives us some of the things that they were taught, the great graded hierarchy of angels, and the mysteries of the heavenly world. And then others speak of these same Mysteries. S. Clement of Alexandria tells us much, tells us much that he says will not be readily understood by all, but they will understand, he says, who have been touched with the thyrsus - the rod of Initiation, the cone-crowned rod, with which every candidate in the Mysteries was touched, by which the sacred fire was set free, so that the eyes were opened and the secrets of the unseen world revealed. Those who have been thus touched, says S. Clement, will understand the allusions that he makes. And much more is told us by Origen - he has not the prefix of Saint, though he well deserved it, because on some points his doctrine was too liberal for the party which became the dominant party of the Church. He tells us much about the teachings, how they were given by the Christ Himself, how they were given in the secrecy of the house after the crowd had gone, to His disciples in the house, quoting the words of the

Gospel. How these teachings were handed down from one to another, never written but always 'from mouth to ear' as the phrase has it, and told only to those who were 'perfect'. The word 'perfect was used for the Initiated. (Some of you may recall that it is used in Modern Masonry, the tradition still alive.) We read also in Origen some of the formulae used, and we learn from him that they who were thus initiated were the Gnostics, the knowers. They *knew,* they not only believed. And he says that no Church could last unless it had the Gnostics an its pillars. It was true that the Church had medicine for the sinner, but it had also knowledge for the wise, and only ' those who knew' could keep the Church safe from attack, and its doctrines safe from degradation. Read, when you have leisure, his wonderful description of the Gnostic and his life. Then you will realize something of the power in the early Church where such Gnostics were the teachers, and where none might pass to the highest grades of the priesthood unless they had passed through the Mysteries and had learned in the presence of others the secrets of the faith, confided to the circle of the perfected. And so we find, looking thus at it from the historical point of view, a succession of stages of teaching. The Christ himself in the body of the disciple, able to stay but for a short time and then slain; the disciple reborn to carry on the work; and, until his re-birth, the great Master himself the Teacher in the sacred circle of His Initiates. Then the travelling far and wide of the great Messenger, the making of occult centers, the preparation for a future then far from the birth, but which we are finding now as the near future. For those secret centers, existing as they do in Europe, are the centers whence the light shall spread, the centers where the Masters shall stand, where disciples shall be gathered, whence the teaching shall go forth.

And so looking, we come on to the time when in the Mysteries the teaching still was given which made the Gnostics of the early Church. Then a great change comes over

Christendom. Christianity and the State embrace, the State wanting to use the religion in order to win wider power for itself, and so making treaty, as it were, with the Church. And then the gradual passing away of the Mysteries, slowly, through the centuries; the gradual withdrawal for want of pupils, and the passing on of the memory of the Mysteries to little scattered bodies of people who, under various titles, carried on the scientific studies which had formed part of the learning of the Mysteries; now and again publishing under mysterious names some of the results of their labor, publishing those strange things called the rosaries, 'under the sign of the rose' the secret sign, giving alchemical and medical mysteries, daring not to speak aloud and plainly, because of the danger.

And so gradually the occult knowledge was veiled more and more deeply, for the blood of the Christ did not fall only on those who shed it nor on the people to whom they belonged. It has fallen as a shadow over the whole of Christendom, hiding the Mysteries; making invisible the occult side of truth. For the persecuting mind awoke, and the prison gaped for those who knew the hidden things of the Spirit, and the lips were silenced and the tongues were rendered dumb, and the outer knowledge was thrown into the form of dogma, and the inner knowledge was proscribed as Gnosticism and heresy. It never died. It was handed on from group to group; the torch of the Wisdom was never wholly extinguished but none dared to speak openly; and so we have come down to our own days where still the veil is thrown over the Mysteries - a veil now to be gradually withdrawn, because once more the feet of the coming Christ are heard, and the world must be prepared for the coming, the thought of the Mysteries must again be a reality. And as during the last thirty years the doctrines that lead to knowledge have been spread far and wide, so now the outcome of those doctrines must be gradually rendered familiar to the minds of men - the great facts of Initiation, not only in

131

books as words, but in life; the fact that Initiation is as possible now as in the far-off past, that men and women pass the portals now as they passed them long ago. And in the coming years you will find gradually more and more will be spoken, more and more will be declared, in order that some of the arrows of skepticism may break on our breasts and be blunted, ere He, the Master of Masters, shall come to face the unbelief of the world. And so you will find gradually we shall talk more and more of these things, and shall talk more and more openly. Let the world mock as it mocked before. Facts do not change because of ridicule. Far better they should mock the servants than the Master. Far better they should ridicule and scoff at the disciples than at their Lord.

Thus you have that historical side reviewed. You should study it, as far as you can. Be willing to reason about it, to discuss it, and do not mix up your feelings with that part of the study.

Next you come to the critical side, the side of the doctrines. There you should try to gain some knowledge, for such knowledge is valuable. How the experiences were written; who wrote them; why they are all written not as the gospel of so-and-so but as the gospel *according* to so-and-so, pointing out the existence of different schools of tradition in the early Church. There was one school of tradition that bore the name of Matthew, others those of Mark, of Luke, and of John, each writer giving the tradition according to a school, named after its head in the eastern way. I think that all now practically admit that the Fourth Gospel - that according to S. John - belongs to the great Neo platonic and Alexandrian school, that it is less the record of a life than the record of a heart and mind. This Gospel is very different in tone from the others, and is quite irreconcilable with them as regards the outline of facts, but it is pregnant with the deepest lessons, full of the most inspiring thought. And just as that Neo-platonic and Alexandrian gospel is said to be 'according to S. John', because in him was more of the mind and heart of the Christ than in any other of the apostles, so the others also are marked as to their origin, and give us the varying traditions which have come down, the story of that wondrous life. Learn something of their value as historical documents. You ought to know something of that as students. And you can study it quietly, indifferent to many points that may be raised, because they do not touch the real Christ but only the authenticity of the particular documents. The proof of the Christ is not in the writings but in His Church, and in the devotion of the ever-growing millions of human hearts, generation after generation, round His feet. Read all criticism fearlessly; it cannot touch aught that is of value.

Then we come to a typo of criticism which does not so much criticize the different documents, though it grows out of that, as challenges the whole conception of this historical Christ. That I think is growing, on the whole, weaker now than it was some thirty years ago, when it was very strong, when Strauss' Life came out, when the idea of the Sun-myth dominated, enormously strengthened by many of the archaeological and antiquarian researches, by the discovery of similar stories round the lives of many Saviors, of identical symbols - like the symbol of the cross, everywhere to be discovered in the ancient world, but rarely in the catacombs where Christians were buried, where it was less frequent as a symbol than others which later dropped out of sight. The crucifix, you will remember, did not appear till about the sixth century after Christ. But the cross existed in the world tens of thousands of years before the birth of the Lord Maitreya as the Christ. On the real meaning of the cross, however, I shall have a word or two to say presently. You have then the idea put forward that the whole so-called history of the Christ grows out of the Sun-myth stories. A mistaken idea, but a profoundly

133

interesting one, because, while the story of the living man did not grow out of the Sun- myth, much of the Sun-myth gathered round the living man and clothed Him in garments that in His own physical life He did not wear. And there lies the interest. A very large amount of the story of the Christ - of the Christ sometimes spoken of as the cosmic Christ or the Second LOGOS - belongs to the great religion of the Sun.

You all know that myth is much more important than history. History is the record - I was going to say of facts, but very often not oven of facts - and it is only that. And a fact, you know, is a very poor little thing when you come to look at it. It is only the fourth or fifth reflection of the great truths in the world of Ideas. When a great Idea is in the heavens, it is thrown downwards into grosser and grosser matter, and each grosser sphere cuts off one aspect of the Idea, and when you have got most of the aspects cut off and the Idea comes down to the physical, you call the fragment a fact. That is what facts are. And you think so much of them. Now the myth is the expression of the Idea as it exists in the heavenly world, and that is always true. It comes down then in the pictorial form, and the picture contains much more than the word, the dogma. The picture of a thing tells you much more than a few words describing it. Put a thought into music, and it tells you more of its beauty than if you only described it. Taint it on canvas, carve it in marble, and more of the Idea comes through than in the mere description. And so with myth. The great myth is the truth that the Second LOGOS, pouring-out His life into the world - He whose body is the Sun - sends that light and life into the world, supporting, maintaining and vivifying. The Sun-worship of the elder days was not only a collection of stories; it was the very life of the Sun, of the God in the Sun, poured down on the worshippers upon earth. It is the oldest and the mightiest of all religions, the religion of our far-off ancestors in Atlantis even; still more beautiful was it in the great City of the Bridge, the inheritance of the Indian Aryas, as given by Vyasa. And that religion taught how the life of God interpenetrates His world, so that every fragment of the world is vitalized by the Divine Life. That it lives by Him, moves in Him, exists in Him, and if He could cease to think it, would pass away like a shadow of a dream.

And then the Elders taught the people how the Sun as symbol passed through the stages, year by year, which marked out the ideal human life. Born into the weakness of childhood, rising into the strength of manhood, giving life for the benefit of humanity, ascending into heaven to pour down blessing upon earth - the story of the Sun-God, They called it. And that you find in every nation; that you find traced fully or partially in the great scriptures of the world. And much of that great story wound itself round the picture of the Christ as the human lineaments faded and the divine shone out from within, until the adoration and the love of His followers could not distinguish between the glory of the Godhead and the glory of the manhood through which it shone, and they called him God, who truly is God manifested in the flesh, not apart from us, but "the first-born among many brethren". For in each of us lives the same Divinity, in germ in us, unfolded splendidly in Him.

So that all that is *true*. And I want you to see it as intellectually true, so that you may not have a difficulty when you hear Him spoken of as the Son of God, the Second Person of the Trinity, the cosmic Christ, the Life of the world. Such Life there is, and such Life is embodied in every Son of Man. Fear not, then, when stress is laid upon that aspect, for it inspires man to effort. And as the light of the sun warms the physical body, so does the light of that divine Sun warm the human heart.

And thus you find a view made into an attack, where it ought to be made as an explanation and an increase of glory. And you find there the first explanation of the Cross. Plato spoke of the WORD, the LOGOS, as marked out on the universe as a Cross. But think a moment of what that Cross is. The universe from the Platonic standpoint was a sphere, and a cross marked upon it was the cross of equal arms, sometimes called the Greek Cross. And the manifestation of the Spirit descending into matter, crucified in matter, is the Cross, the equal-armed Cross, the. Cross of the Spirit, first marked on, then submerged, then triumphant, in matter.

As this thought spread, the Sun-God and the Cross became identified. And the life of the Spirit outpoured upon the world had as its symbol this equal-armed Cross. Then, coming downwards, that is represented in the Mysteries. And inasmuch as it had to be represented pictorially, after the power to make living forms had passed because of ignorance, the Mysteries became a drama which was acted, and then the Sun-God no longer appeared triumphant on the sphere in space, but outstretched on the cross of matter, crucified in matter, and you have no longer the equal-armed cross but the Latin cross, one arm lengthened that the body of the man crucified may be thereon represented. And so the mystic teaching grew up, and all still gathered round the splendid figure of the Christ. And out of that mystic teaching, the teaching of the Mysteries, in which the body was crucified that the Spirit might triumph, the lower self sacrificed to the higher that the higher might reign triumphant over the matter that was thereby redeemed - because of that, this double cross came into Christendom from-the far-off past, the Cross of the Passion and the Cross of the Spirit triumphant.

And that in the truest sense is myth, the great spiritual truth, higher than all fact, and over represented in the history of the human Spirit. And Christ crucified is that magnificent ideal in which man arises triumphant, having crucified the lower self on the cross of matter; the body is dead and buried, and then the Christ arises triumphant from the sepulcher, bearing on His banner the equal-armed Cross of the Spirit that has triumphed, that has made matter the servant of the Spirit, and has redeemed the body by making it the subject of the Spirit - that wondrous, ever-true myth of Christ, to be re-lived by you and by me, if ever we would attain to the place of the Spirit triumphant.

And then, studying, we learn to understand, and we realize, as is generally the case, that there is a truth embodied in each conception, and that what we want is the power to link the truths together and see them in their full, all-round perfection, instead of in their fragmentary aspects. And so we learn that the historical story of the man Christ Jesus is true, and that such a Mighty One indeed has lived and taught upon our earth; and that the story of the Sun-god is true, and that a far higher, even the eternal Christ, comes ever down and lives in men, in order that the whole world of men may be redeemed and spiritualized; and that the story of the Mysteries is true, in which every human Spirit re-treads the path and re-lives the story, and in his turn becomes a Christ, first crucified, and then triumphant. So that instead of quarrelling with any, we stretch out hands of welcome towards all, for all bring us a fragment of the truth, and all the truths join together into the perfect picture of the Christ that is the Object of worship.

On the dogmatic Christ I have not much time to dwell. But I will remind you that in the controversies which rent the early Church there were two especially: one which disputed - as though anyone could know anything about it - whether the Christ was of one substance with God or of like substance, whether in the eternal relation of that triple LOGOS one poor human word was more accurate than another in the efforts to describe. Over that the Church split, with the satisfaction of feeling that the severed parts could never come together again, because the question could never be decided. None save God Himself can know the mysteries of His own nature. And who are we to curse our brethren, because they see those mysteries at an angle a little different from our own? And then there came the great controversy which cast the Gnostics out of the Church, and made it neither Catholic nor Gnostic, neither universal nor knowing, because the Catholic cannot exclude, and the non- Gnostic cannot know. The part of the Church left had no right to the name of Catholic, having cast out the other.

The Gnostics taught, as we teach today, that the body of the disciple was used for the indwelling Spirit of the Christ. There is nothing new and mysterious about that. I was told the other day in a letter that this was one of the secrets of the inner teaching, but that some of the outer people knew it. I answered that it would be very odd if they did not, seeing that the Gnostics taught it in the early centuries of the Church. Do not make mysteries where there are none. This duality, Jesus and Christ, is a very, very old idea. The Manichaeans hold it, among many others. It is quite common and well-known to every scholar. And it happens to be true. And so today we have to say it over again. And because it has been long forgotten, it startles people. Lecturing once to an audience of the clergy, I found that they almost all knew about it. It was a heresy they said - which I admitted - but a heresy is only the belief of the minority. But in any case it is only an intellectual question and not of vital importance, certainly not worth quarrelling about.

Now what is of importance? First the Ideal - the ideal of a perfect humanity irradiated with Divinity, so irradiated that you cannot say which is God and which is man, the seed of Divinity having flowered into perfection, the spark of Divinity

138

having blazed out into a dazzling fire. That matters. That is the Ideal: the perfect man become the manifestation of the perfect God. As said the Christ: " Be ye perfect even as your Father in heaven is perfect." And to realize that that has been done, to know that that has been achieved, that such splendor of manhood has arisen that we cannot tell it from Godhead, that is the Ideal of the Christ. And that is all important. You name that Ideal Christ. In the East they give him other names. But the names do not matter. It is the thought that counts. Call him Christ, or Buddha, or what you will, but do not quarrel over the name, lest the dust raised by the quarrel should cloud the sunlight of the Ideal.

I speak of Him here as the Christ, because that name represents to you that perfect Example who lived in Judea and is the center of the Christian Church. But speaking to the Hindu I use the Hindu name, to the Buddhist, the Buddhist name; for I would not by a name blind the eyes, and as it were lock with a name the door of the heart which should open to the coming of the Lord. The names matter not; He answers to them all. And there is only One who bears all these names, the Supreme Teacher of the world. He is One. And it is to Him we look, no matter by what name we call Him. Our prayers reach Him, no matter how we address the outside envelope of the prayer. That is the Ideal that I would pray you to keep.

But you will lose it, if you quarrel about it. You cannot see it, if you dispute over it. It is too sacred for dispute; it is the vision of the intuition, not the result of reasoning. And reason must be silent when intuition speaks, for intuition sees where reason only argues. And that is the Ideal on which you should daily think, because thought is creative and transforms the thinker into the likeness of that on which he thinks; after that, then turn your will and your heart to reproducing in yourself some fragment of that life. Take it as an inspiration, as a thing to brood over, rather than to talk about. For much strength of the Spirit goes out in the spoken words, and those who speak too much have often little strength remaining wherewith to live and to act. Emotions are wasted in too much expression, and you need to learn to restrain them, so that they may be a mighty force to be used in the service of the Highest when He needs them for His work. And if to you the Christ be the great Ideal, the constant inspiration, then you will feel the truth of that phrase I have often used: "The LOGOS of the soul is one." There, there is no division. There, no doubt arises. There, all that is strong and beautiful and splendid unites in one perfect image - the image of Christ the Lord.

And how beautiful to think that when the Hindu thinks along these lines, he sees the One he calls the Jagat Guru, the World-Teacher, and sees Him as you see Him, and feels to Him as you feel to Him, and has been taught to say that "whatever form a man worships, I give the faith that worships that form." And, "If anyone offers a flower, a drop of water with faith, he worships Me." Thus is the Hindu taught to see the many aspects of the Divine. And when the Buddhist thinks, he thinks the same, loves the same, and worships the same, although he gives again a different name. And so the world's love goes up in one voice supreme, beginning as many and uniting in one great chord, to the Supreme Teacher, the Receiver of all love and the Giver of all help.

And that thought in what I call the Holy of Holies, where no voice of controversy should be heard. That is why I ask you to give to the intellect the things of the intellect, but to offer the things of the Spirit in the heart of the Spirit. Let us study all views about the Christ. Something will be learned from all of them, for He is too mighty for one man's mouth to express Him, for one pen to write the fullness of His manifold perfection. Study them all, and learn something from each. But

140

when you turn to the Christ Himself, let controversies die, and rise to the height of the Ideal. We have an eastern fashion that, when we go into the house of a man, much more into the Temple of the God, we put off outside the door the shoes that are covered with the dust of the road along which we have walked, and entering with pure feet, without soil of dust, we greet the friend, or worship the God. Let us do thus with the ideal Christ. Put off the shoes of controversy when you approach Him, for the place on which you stand is holy ground. Let the dust of earth remain on the cast-off shoes, and enter with pure feet and heart aflame with love into the presence of the Holiest, who is the Eternal Peace and Love. So shall the Christ remain to you the holiest name on earth; so shall you cling to all the sacred memories which from your babyhood have entwined themselves round that holiest of names; and you shall meet your Hindu brother, your Buddhist brother, your Hebrew brother, your Parsi brother, and find that you all worship the same Teacher, and can talk heart to heart and Spirit with Spirit, knowing that the Lord is One.

And so I would leave you with my message for the coming year, to be repeated whenever controversy arises, or when any would attack your thought or assert his own. Take as the year a watchword that phrase I have so often quoted, place it in the mouth of the Supreme Teacher: "On whatsoever road a man approaches Me, on that road do I welcome him, for all roads are Mine."

The Rosicrucians and the Alchemists

by Florence Farr

A legend arose in the time of the Lutheran outburst of a mysterious master called Christian Rosenkreutz, who was buried for a period of all years in the central cavern of the earth. His shrine was seven-sided, and all the symbols of the universe were said to have been found disposed round him in this place. The Egyptian tradition of Seker, the god in the central cavern of the Duat, evidently found an echo in the heart of the inventor of this legendary father of mysteries, and it will be interesting to try and discern the meanings of the main symbols of the Rosenkreutz legends in Egypt and in Germany.

The Egyptian Duat, or Underworld, was represented by a five-fold star, or star of five radiations, enlarging as they receded from the center, and therefore not bearing the same symbolism as the pentagram. The Rose is fivefold in its structure and is a well-known symbol of silence. The stages of its existence pass from the bud, or potential state of pralaya, to the unfolding of its leaves as the pleroma, or fulness or manifestation of creative power. Consciousness, thought, reasoning, will, and the sense of individuality are five of its powers; the five senses are other manifestations of the same symbol. When the pollen of a flower is ripe the creative work begins, the petals fall and the fruit and seed are formed. The processes of life are a rhythmic coiling and uncoiling; a radiation and attraction, and an emanation or separation. The fruit coils round the seeds, the juices pass to and fro, and finally the husk of the fruit bursts and the seeds fall out separately as emanations, each complete in itself.

So, in the degrees of human enlightenment the purest state is Being so unified and perfect that the kind of consciousness that depends upon comparison cannot exist. The second state is the sense of being without bounds, which is often called wisdom. The third state is discernment, or understanding, and may be attained by concentration of the subjective mind upon an object until full understanding is attained. And these states of the unmanifest consciousness are called Sat-Chit-Ananda in the Vedantic philosophy and Ain-Soph-Aur in the Kabalistic philosophy; and Ptah-Seker-Osiris was the concrete image of these ideas in Egypt.

Now the Rose of the Rosicrucians was a more complicated symbol than the Cup. As we have seen the Cup was a symbol of creation, and its form was connected with the symbol of a circle in contrast to the Cross. The symbol of the Rose contains five petals and five divisions of the calyx. It is evidently the symbol of creation in activity, not in potentiality only. Perhaps we may believe the Rose to be a symbol of the subtle body of man, which is one with nature, and the Cross the symbol of the body and the name of word of man. The union of the Rose and Cross would symbolize a man able to unite himself to the great powers of Nature, or tattvas, familiar to us under their Hindu names Akasa, Vayu, Tejas, Apas and Prithivi, or the kingdoms of sound, sensation, perception. absorption and reproduction more commonly called hearing, touching, seeing, eating and generating.

Now the notion of obtaining the natural powers of an adept is most apparent in the traditions that come through Egypt and Chaldea, and the idea of the super-essential state in contrast to power is most apparent in the Oriental traditions. The high caste Oriental has the aristocratic spirit that conceives the height of life on this world to consist in the delicacy of perception associated with perfect self-satisfaction, while the democratic spirit of the West cannot conceive itself without desires, struggles and potencies for gratifying desires; democracy wishes to do and to have; aristocracy is sufficient unto itself.

Rosicrucianism and Alchemy are both allegories constructed by these working democratic minds, and in the alchemical symbolism we can trace the exact degrees of initiation through which the man, still under the great race delusion of progress, must pass before he realizes that his real self is the same yesterday, today and forever.

It is true in a sense that this treasure of all sages, this knowledge of Being which all mystics seek, forms itself vehicles in time and space in which it carries out the imaginations which spring from the relative side of absolute consciousness, and it is interesting to trace the different degrees of attainment.

Alchemical symbolism is mainly the symbolism of distillation. To take a simple process, let us imagine that we desire to obtain the white and the red tinctures from honey. The alchemist would put the honey in the cucurbite of an alembic. Placing it over a gentle heat he would drive the essential part of the spirit into the head or beak of the alembic, whence it would pass as steam into the neck of the receiver and become liquid once more as it cooled. This liquid was the white tincture, or spirit of honey mixed with water. This is the symbol of that concentration and meditation whereby the mind of man becomes subtilized and fit to perceive philosophical impressions. The white tincture is the symbol of light and wisdom.

But to obtain the red tincture of power a far more complicated process had to be performed. It consisted mainly of pouring back the distilled spirit upon the black dead-head that had been left as residue in the cucurbite and by the exercise of great care and the addition of certain matters acting upon the mixture in such a way that finally the whole of the original matter was distilled and no black dead-head remained and a wonderful red tincture was the result of the transmutation of the black nature.

This symbolical process involves the passing through definite stages of progress in the world of changing life. Let us imagine it carried out to its logical conclusion upon our own earth. We know that the mineral kingdom is the state in which form lasts for infinite ages and can stand great heat and cold without destruction. We know that the giants of the vegetable kingdom last many hundreds of years, but although the process of their growth and decay is prolonged, they are not capable of resisting fire or of existing in the frozen zone. We know that certain animals, such as elephants, tortoises and parrots, live for very long periods of time. All these creatures have greater tenacity of existence in the forms or vehicles of life than the human creature.

It is also plain that as the earth becomes more and more subject to violent change, when the great floods and the ice and the burnings visit it, in its old age conscious life must exist in more enduring but less complex, sensitive, visible forms than it does at present. Now consciousness of Being is the name we give to the white tincture which the adept distils from his human form in the alembic of the mind. It is brought about by the fire of imagined emotion and devotion under the stress of intense concentration. To focus thought has the same effect as to focus sunlight. It becomes a force analogous to heat. It is, in a word, emotion evoked by the skill of the sage. In this fire the Adept raises his consciousness until it is separate from the gross body, and no longer aware of the objective world. Passing through the gate of dreams it enters the subjective world and lives in its own brightness. Here it learns that it can create infinite visions and glories, and here the saints rejoice, each in his own heaven. Here finally the sage perceives his own divinity and is united to his God. This is the white initiation in the eyes of the Rosicrucian doctors, and according to the scriptures of the alchemists the sage has gained the white tincture. The objective world only remains in his consciousness as blackness and ignorance and death. In his divine nature he seeks to redeem the dark world, to draw it up into the divine nature and make it perfect. His vision can now show him a world in which man can no longer exist in material human form. His own desire for wisdom has drawn up the human element out of the visible or objective state. He is no longer merely a man in a human body because his subtle body has possessed itself of the characteristic human faculty of self-conscious comparison, the origin of wit, laughter and criticism.

The humanity that is beyond animal consciousness has the power of acting and knowing at the same moment; it can seem one thing and know at the same time that it is another. It is not a noble quality; it is nothing more than the power of laughing at ourselves: and yet it is the great redeeming quality, for it is the germ of all wisdom and enlightenment.

The ordinary dreamer lives in his subtle body as the fool of his own fancy, and the dream shows how little human wisdom his subtle body has obtained: but the subtle body of an adept can perceive the illusionary formulation of panoramas of light and form arising from the half-seized impression of light falling at a certain angle across the red edge of a blanket and the linen of a sheet just as he closes his eyes. The dream of the sage is a consciously guided dream. Like an author, he writes his own dramas and delights in the joys and tragedies of his creation, He no longer suffers from the attacks and sorrows that his own mind creates, but observes them with excitement and interest. He watches his own tears and cuts into the heart of his own emotions.

These are some of the experiences of the sage who has transferred the human principle from the body of matter to the subtle body.

The material body may in this stage of enlightenment be considered as a beautiful and healthy animal; it carries on the physical functions in temperate ways, unaccompanied by the fantastic imaginations of a human being. And there is little doubt that the bull of Apis was considered to take the place of the body of the adept Osiris in this way. The body of a sacred animal would answer every purpose for the divine man whose invisible body had attained some degree of complex, conscious life. The nervous forces of the animal world act as the physical basis for the dream-powers of the subtilized or deified man.

In China the flying dragon, the mythical combination of all kinds of animal life, represents the body of the deified man that can command all the elemental states of matter that can exist in the air, the fire, the earth and the water. The dragon is the symbol of the material body of the being who has complete command of the elemental world and afterwards becomes the subtle body in the further stage of being of which we are told in Druid tradition.

When the earth grows older and complex animal forms such as flying-fish and sea-serpents and monstrous alligators, can no longer exist, another symbol must be taken from the writings of the Rosicrucian doctors and the alchemists, and we enter upon the study of the Tree of Life. He who eats of the fruit of the Tree of Life will become one with the Elohim, or creative gods, and will live for infinite ages.

Imagine the world enveloped in a great white cloud, moist and warm like a hot-house; giant palms and ferns and mosses dripping with moisture: a climate like that of the Cocoa-palm Islands off the west coast of Africa, where animals and men can only live a little time. In this world the adept would use some marvelous tree as the physical basis of his life: and his subtle body would have drawn up into itself all the forces of motion that make a tree less powerful to our minds than an animal. The subtle body in this state would have become a veritable dragon of complex forces. It would have drawn into itself the mixed sphinx-natures of the birds and the fish, the creeping things and the four-footed creatures. The dryad of each tree would be a mighty Druid; the great Pendragon would have his oak as a physical form and would exercise his power in reality as we can imagine the ancient Druid sages exercised theirs in imagination.

This state of the subtle body may perhaps have been symbolized by the Green Dragon of the alchemists, but the Red Dragon arose after still further distillation.

Now we have to imagine a world all fire and molten glory of flame, in which no tree or flower could exist; a world in which wonderful agate trees would circle the white crystals of their pith with bands of violet and hyacinth and blue melting into stretches of pale chalcedony and shrouded in dark crystal bark, their branches glimmering with emerald leaves; a world in which mineral life has learned at last to show itself in perfect form, where light and fire glowed alternately and played with elemental shapes and images of beauty. And so, at last, we come to the last symbol of the alchemists – the symbol of the final perfection, the Summum Bonum, the Philosopher's Stone.

Let us imagine what that state would mean for the adept; his gross body a pure ruby, a perfect crystalline form with all the powers of growth, of nourishment, of reproduction drawn from the vegetable kingdom into his subtle body, carried on without disgust or satiety through the beautiful mediums of fiery blossoms and shining leaves; his subtle body almost visible as a light shining in the fiery world; his children flowers of flame and his physical form an everlasting memory of beauty; his mind an all-pervading consciousness in which blossoming imaginations arose or subsided under the law of his will; a perception unified with a faculty that ordered joy to succeed sorrow and sorrow to succeed joy because he knew that one cannot manifest without the other. A supreme artist, he would rejoice in creation; a supreme critic, he would rejoice in contrast.

So, the red tincture would be attained and the black, the white and the red worlds explored and analyzed in the imagination of the Rosicrucians and alchemists of the Middle Ages.

We still see the same desire for progress among those who strive for the ancient stone here in this western democratic world of men who desire "to have" and "to do." But these circles of everlasting recurrence so dear to Friedrich Nietzche are not what he called them. They are not aristocratic.

The aristocracy of mind is shown in the philosophy of Villiers de l'Isle Adam, who cried: "As for living, our servants can do that for us." It is the feeling of the great Buddhist intellect who sees that in the words "I am not" there is a wonder and a vision and song far exceeding the mere ideas of limited ecstasy and knowledge concealed in the words "I am."

Aphorisms From the East

by Helena P. Blavatsky

Two things are impossible in this world of Maya: to enjoy more than Karma hath allotted; to die before one's hour hath struck.

-oOo-

A student without inclination for work is like a squirrel on its wheel; he makes no progress.

-oOo-

A traveler without observation is a bird without wings.

-oOo-

A learned man without pupils, is a tree which bears no fruit; a devotee without good works, is a dwelling without a door.

-oOo-

When Fate overtakes us, the eye of Wisdom becomes blind.

-oOo-

Keep thine eyes open, or Fate will open them for thee.

-oOo-

He who kisses the hand he cannot cut off, will have his head cut off by the hand he now kisses in the next rebirth.

-oOo-

He who keeps to his business, he who loves his companions, he who does his duty, will never be poor.

-oOo-

A thousand regrets will not pay thy debts.

-oOo-

Fallen flowers do not return to their stems, nor departed friends to their houses.

-oOo-

To feel one's ignorance is to be wise; to feel sure of one's wisdom is to be a fool.

-oOo-

One proof is better than ten arguments.

-oOo-

Rain in the morn brings the sun after noon. He who weeps today, may laugh tomorrow.

-oOo-

The soothsayer for evil never knows his own fate.

-oOo-

Like oil, truth often floats on the surface of the lie. Like clear water, truth often underlies the seeming falsehood.

-oOo-

Often vinegar got for nothing, is sweeter to the poor man than honey bought.

-oOo-

Every tree hath its shadow, every sorrow its joy.

-oOo-

The fields are damaged by weeds, mankind by passion. Blessed are the patient, and the passionless.

-oOo-

The virtuous man who is happy in this life, is sure to be still happier in his next.

-oOo-

What ought to be done is neglected, what ought not to be done is done. The sins of the unruly are ever increasing.

-oOo-

Without Karma, no fisherman could catch a fish; outside of Karma, no fish would die on dry land, or in boiling water.

-oOo-

Let every man first become himself that which he teaches others to be.

-oOo-

He who hath subdued himself, may hope to subdue others. One's own self is the most difficult to master.

-oOo-

Hatred is never quenched by hatred; hatred ceases by showing love; this is an old rule.

-oOo-

The path of virtue lies in the renunciation of the seven great sins.

-oOo-

The best possession of the man of clay is health; the highest virtue of the man of spirit is truthfulness.

-oOo-

Man walks on, and Karma follows him along with his shadow.

-oOo-

Daily practical wisdom consists of four things: — To know the root of Truth, the branches of Truth, the limit of Truth, and the opposite of Truth.

Symbolism of the Serpent

by Sarah F. Gordon

Mystics see in the Serpent the emblem of Cosmic Force, a high spiritual essence whose influence pervades the realm of matter.

The emblem of Eternity is a Serpent with its tail in its mouth: a circle, never beginning, never ending. It also represents the Astral Light or Universal Soul from which all that exists is born by separation or differentiation. Through all space thrill the magnetic and electrical elements of animate Nature, the life- giving and death-giving, for life on one plane is death on another plane. In the Secret Doctrine, it says: — "That 'Mystery of the Serpent' was this: Our Earth, or rather *terrestrial life,* is often referred to in the Secret Teachings as the great Sea, 'the sea of life' having remained to this day a favorite metaphor. The *Siphrah Dtzenioutha* speaks of primeval chaos and the evolution of the Universe after a destruction (pralaya), comparing it to an uncoiling serpent: — 'Extending hither and thither, its tail in its mouth, the head twisting on its neck, it is enraged and angry. ... It watches and conceals itself. *Every Thousand Days* it is manifested' "

In the Kabala, the creative Force makes sketches and spiral lines in the shape of a serpent. It holds its tail in its mouth, the symbol of endless eternity and of cyclic periods.

It is held that the ancients believed more in the spiritual or invisible powers of Nature than the men of the present day. Spirit and Matter were opposite poles of the same essence. The dual is in all, active and passive, male and female. The nearer to the heart of Mother Nature man keeps, the more he comprehends spiritual truths. A symbol once adopted is kept by its sacredness, though with varying meanings according to that which is uppermost in the mind of the user. Hence a knowledge of the soul life of races is the only true guide in the explanation of symbols. The symbolic hieroglyphics of the ancients were based upon the occult science of correspondences. They defended symbolic teaching on the ground that the symbol left so much unexplained that thereby the intellect was stimulated and trained to deep thinking. Often, alas, the reverse is seen; the symbol being accepted as the thing itself. Occultism teaches that the possible in *thought* is possible in *action*. Religion rests on a mental want, we hope, we fear, because we desire. Both emotions prompt action and, to that extent, are opposed to thought. Religion has been through all the forms of self-love, sex-love, love of country, love of humanity, while in each is the germ of the highest love. Develop very strongly any of these forms of love and it will concentrate whatever religious aspirations a person has. All point to one high form which can become a passion for truth. "By the Divine Power of Love all Nature becomes renewed." This is the secret which underlies all the symbols. "Right thought is the path to Life Everlasting: those who think do not die," is an old philosophical axiom. Goethe said "Confidence and resignation, the sense of subjection to a higher will which rules the course of events but which we do not fully comprehend, are the fundamental principles of every better religion."

The Occultist believes that the spiritual and psychic involution proceed on parallel lines with physical evolution; that the inner senses were innate in the first human races.

The serpent is the symbol of the Adept, of his powers of Divine Knowledge. It is the emblem of wisdom and prudence. Every people revered the symbol. Jesus acknowledged the great wisdom and prudence of the serpent. "Be ye wise as serpents." The serpent also symbolizes the creative power. The creative powers in man are the gift of Divine Wisdom, not the result of sin. The curse was not pronounced for seeking natural union, but for abusing these powers. Thus arose good and evil. This is the real curse alluded to in Genesis.

It is owing to the serpent being oviparous that it becomes a symbol of wisdom and an emblem of the Logoi or the Self-born. The *egg* was chosen as the universal symbol on account of its form and its inner mystery. Within the closed shell evolved a living creature apparently self-created.

The serpent represents the sensual, magnetic element which fascinates while it causes ruin: the alluring of the spiritual force into the vortex of sentient existence. By the symbol of the serpent the ancients represented fire, light, life, struggle, effort, thought, consciousness, progress, civilization, liberty, independence; at the same time it is the ever revolving circle with its opposite poles, life and death, pleasure and pain, heat and cold, light and darkness, active and passive. With heat comes expansion and consequent disintegration into new forms of life. It is only through sentient manifestation that man can rise to the plane of life immortal. It is in the experience earned through the tortures of mortality that man may evolve a God. No spiritual and psychic evolution is possible on earth for one who is forever passive. That would be failure on this material plane. Man is born, he has to evolve the angel by long and repeated lives on earth. Human passions correspond to the earth, which is the fructifier of the seed or germ sown in its depths. As the Voice of the Silence says: — "Out of the furnace of man's life and its black smoke, winged flames arise, flames purified, that, soaring onward 'neath the Karmic eye, weave in

the end the fabric glorified of the three vestures of the Path."
"Inaction based on selfish fear can bear but evil fruit. The
selfish devotee lives to no purpose. The man who does not go
through his appointed work in life has lived in vain."

"Follow the wheel of life, follow the wheel of duty to
race and kin, to friend and foe, and close thy mind to pleasures
as to pain. Both action and inaction may find room in thee, thy
body agitated, thy mind tranquil, thy soul as limpid as a
mountain lake."

The Reality of Dream-Consciousness

by Mabel Collins

"A good many people believe in the reality of the dream-life, in the wandering of the disembodied spirit." These words are spoken by Michael Ossory, the hero of H. A. Vachell's novel, *The Face of Clay.*

The present writer, who is one of the "good many people," holds that they have as good a case, if not a better one, than those who believe that dreams are mere fantasies. In an article in the *British Medical Journal* of August 18, 1906, the following sentence occurs: "Everyone must have been struck at some time or another, when waking from a dream, by the extra ordinary fidelity with which places and things have been represented, the stage properties having been reproduced in the dream with a luxuriance and minute exactitude only vainly emulated in waking moments."

This well represents the attitude taken by materialistic thinkers, and nothing can be said in answer to it without introducing the great question raised in the second part of Michael Ossory's remark. To those who hold that there is nothing but the physical world, and that a man cannot experience anything except through the medium of his physical body, dreams are but illusions. Yet even they are compelled to admit, as does the writer in the *British Medical Journal,* that the vividness and intensity of dream-consciousness is extraordinary. He is referring to scenes and details which are stored in the memory, but he goes on to say, "Memories long lost to waking consciousness have been rescued from oblivion in this way, and so have details which did not seem ever to have been consciously observed." Many who, believing in the wandering of the disembodied spirit, are not so cautious in expressing themselves as a materialistic writer must of necessity be, would readily recall and record instances in which not only were details seen in dream-consciousness which had never been observed in waking hours, but also details utterly unlike anything ever seen or to be seen in those hours. Details, yes, and whole scenes, pageants, events which could not by any means be described in ordinary language. All who make a practice of endeavoring to recollect their dream-life are encountered by this extraordinary circumstance of, from time to time, remembering something which is altogether indescribable.

The Essenes regarded that which takes place during the hours of sleep as the most important of the occurrences in the life of the human spirit; they spoke of the waking hours as the period in between, which was filled up by various pursuits. But the night, when the disembodied spirit is free to wander, was the time of true life and progress and education.

In a recent correspondence on "Dreams" in the *Daily Telegraph,* one of the most noticeable things was the constant inquiry: "What does this dream mean?" This is also the most constant remark made in ordinary conversation, if a dream is mentioned or discussed. Why should a dream mean anything? It is a fragmentary recollection of a piece of experience. We all remember the experiences of our waking hours in a fragmentary way; but, no one expects them to "mean anything." Looking back over a week, most people would recall only one or two of the events of each day; but because the rest are forgotten there is no reason to suppose that the ones which are remembered "mean anything."

It is accepted by certain schools of occultism that there are nine states of consciousness to which ordinary human nature can attain; above these is the true mystical state of consciousness, to which the adepts have access. "Dreaming" and "dreamless sleep" are two of these states. In the condition of dreamless sleep, the disembodied spirit has wandered so far afield —beyond the fields of Ardat and the Elysian meadows— that it is not possible for it to bring back anything which the limited human brain is capable of understanding or of recording. Dreaming is a simpler state, ranking next to the waking consciousness. That which is done, experienced, or seen in this state can be conveyed, more or less intelligibly, across the mysterious threshold which separates one consciousness from another. But most of it is lost by the way; the spirit has to make a definite and conscious effort to bring anything clear and coherent, and the brain generally refuses to retain it for long. Everyone knows the sensation of waking with a vivid recollection of a dream-experience, and holding fast to it for a short time only; suddenly the memory of it begins to slip away and the brain can hold it no longer. The power of retaining such memories is one which can be cultivated by concentration upon it, and by effort.

In dreaming-consciousness comes that which all students of occultism so ardently desire—the teacher, the guide. It is common for people to remember doing or seeing something very extraordinary in a dream, by the help of an invisible friend who stood beside them, ready to give aid or to answer questions, but unnoticed unless needed. It seems quite natural that he should be there; just as the child who is learning to walk regards it as quite natural that it should have help.

In the Yoga Aphorisms of Patanjali, six modes are described by which distractions may be combatted. The paragraph in which one of these is given runs as follows: "*Or, by dwelling on knowledge that presents itself in a dream, steadiness of mind may be procured."*

The teacher goes on to say that the student whose mind is thus steadied obtains a mastery which extends from the Atomic to the Infinite. It is with the object of progress and development that the occultist endeavors to bring memories of the dreaming-consciousness into the waking-consciousness, and devotes periods of concentration to this effort. To recall the events which have taken place during the hours of sleep at all intelligently means a blending of the consciousnesses, and sometimes this is keenly realized. I will quote an instance to show what I mean.

"I had long been accustomed to a touch on my forehead as the signal for sleep; insomnia, which threatened to ruin my health, was cured by this help from the invisible. Sometimes it came immediately on my lying down, sometimes not until after long hours of wakefulness. It was like a summons— I was gone instantly, no matter when it came. One night, when the longed-for touch came, to my surprise I remained where I was, but a keen, most delightful consciousness was added to the physical one. The first strange feeling was that the bed in which I lay began to rock gently to and fro, and I clung to it with something of a feeling of alarm at first, till I found that the movement was very gentle, though so decided. I was conscious of my bed, and that I lay in it; but I became aware that at the same time I lay in a boat and that the water on which it moved so softly was warm. How I knew this I cannot tell— I knew it in the curious way one does know things in dreams. I certainly did not put my hand into it, for I clung with both hands to that which was the bed, or the boat. For the first time I had been taken from the waking to the dreaming-consciousness without the dropping of the veil between. How wonderful that was! I fully realized it. The room in which my bed stood was dark and rather chill; my

162

boat was in an atmosphere of warmth and softness and sweetness. I knew there was sunshine, though I could not see it— I could feel, but I had no sight. Suddenly I heard birds— I knew that they were flying, though I could not see them— quantities of birds; those of the same kind sang together, the different kinds following each other according to a law of melody which was outside and beyond anything I could have imagined, as was the effect it produced. I cannot describe it or give any idea of it. Flocks of birds passed in succession across the sky over my head, singing in unison as they went. I tried eagerly to sit up in the boat and look at them, but I had no sight, and very little strength, for I sank back into a state of unconsciousness in which both bed and boat vanished from me. But evidently a guide or teacher was helping me to the attainment of the double consciousness, for I was brought back, from I know not where, by a sharp blow on the side of my bed. It woke me. I was in my bed, beside which stood an invisible form in the darkness—and immediately I was also in the rocking boat on the water, in a place where there was abundant light, which I realized, though I could not open my eyes to it. But, blind though I was, I knew that my boat was close to the shore, and that the same figure which stood beside my bed to summon me, stood on the shore, at the edge of the water, and called to me; and I rose and was helped to leave the boat. I passed away then into experiences which took place beyond the dreaming-consciousness."

The value of that dream lies solely in its clearness, as illustrating the different states. It would "mean nothing" to one who is not a student.

Precious Stones and Their Occult Powers

by Mary L. Lewes

In these enlightened days, many of us feel rather incredulous when we hear of certain curative and protective virtues formerly supposed to be inherent in precious stones, and we are apt to think, that though interesting and curious to read about, such beliefs ought certainly to come under the heading of ancient and mediaeval superstition. This is the very general idea that Dr. Fernie has set himself to modify, in his book entitled *Precious Stones,* a volume which everyone interested in old world-lore, as well as students of the occult, should read with pleasure. The author aims principally to show by his simple and lucid scientific explanations, that the Wise Men of old, and the mediaeval astrologers, had really a sound basis of reason for their belief in the curative powers of certain gems. Though as regards the doctors and quacks of the Middle Ages, it is probable that most of them were ignorant of the real nature of these powers; laying stress only on the ceremonies of magic and sorcery in which their advice as to the wearing of precious stones was involved.

So, from Dr. Femie we learn why the wearing of a diamond may inspire courage; how it is possible that amethysts may indeed soothe and calm the nerves; and why a turquoise worn by certain people loses its color or turns green. And apart from the main object of the book, we are led along innumerable and delightful by-paths of information connected with precious stones; no point of view being omitted that could afford fresh interest or throw new light on the subject.

In his opening chapter the author remarks on the extra ordinary fascination that jewels have from time immemorial exercised over the minds of men and women: a fascination greater than the mere pleasure afforded the eye by the color and luster of stones. Dr. Fernie thinks that perhaps psychometry, which "implies a supposed power of the human mind to discern the past history of inanimate objects by occult telepathic perception," may very probably be concerned with the subtle influence exercised by gems. And to illustrate this theory a most interesting account is given of a series of experiments conducted by Professor Denton with the help of his wife and sister. The whole instance is far too long to quote here, but a few lines will give an idea of the experimenter's object. *"It was the habit of the Professor to select a geological specimen . . . or some fragment of a structure possessing historical interest, and to submit the same to his hypnotized coadjutors, so as to elicit their version of its history. His wife would then readily enter a partially subjective condition of mind, so that—the relic being placed on her head—she would at once pronounce a very plausible and often wonderfully accurate history of the scenes which had been enacted in its ancient environment . . ."* To eliminate any chance of geological knowledge on his wife's part which might possibly be subjectively reproduced, the Professor would hand her specimens so wrapped up that she could not know the contents; and he would also make up several packets so alike that he himself did not know what each contained when he gave them to her. But the result under all tests was the same, *"each specimen handed to Mrs. Denton was described with the same accuracy as before."*

The writer of this article has quoted thus at length from the foregoing passage in Dr. Fernie's book, because she thinks the idea illustrated in the experiments, of telepathic perception furnished by the objects themselves, may give an explanation of some curious phenomena associated with a ring belonging to a lady well known to her, who shall be called Miss Carr. This ring, of obviously antique workmanship, is set with a large jasper stone and resembles a man's signet ring; but the stone has no engraving. Miss Carr relates that some time ago, a friend who came to stay with her found the ring accidentally left in a drawer in her room; and handling it with some curiosity, she looked at the stone rather intently, and presently saw a vision of a street in an Eastern city, and a "man like an Arab" sitting under a palm-tree. It should be added that this lady had never seen nor heard of the ring before, and so was absolutely ignorant of its history. It came originally from an old Arab in Egypt, who declared it to be a talisman against all diseases, and called it "the Stone of the Prophet, picked up near Mecca." On another occasion, Miss Carr, wearing the ring, attended a lecture on occult subjects, and the professor who lectured was shown Miss Carr's ring, and, holding it, said it had a strong sense of protection, and that its owner ought always to wear it. Later in the same evening, while Miss Carr was in a crowd of people, a lady, whom she did not know, came and said to her, "I see a tall Arab dressed in white, with a violet heart on his breast, following you about." Very much astonished by this remark, Miss Carr, after a short conversation, told this lady about her Egyptian ring, and she replied that "the Arab" was probably the former owner of the talisman, and was there to protect her. In relating this story Miss Carr added, "She did not know I possessed the ring until I told her." Of course, both these people so strangely affected by this ring must have been strongly gifted with clairvoyant power; and there is the possibility that their visions *may* have come to them from subjective knowledge unconsciously obtained from Miss Carr's mind. But certainly, in the first case, it almost seems as if it must have been the ring itself which inspired the vision, for when it was found by her friend in the drawer, Miss Carr herself was not present. Can it be indeed, that as Dr. Fernie suggests, "Gems and precious stones retain within themselves a faithful record . . . of physical conditions, and acquired properties, from

167

the primitive time of their original molecular beginning; and that if we allow a suspension for the while, of the wearer's ordinary perceptions . . . the precious stone in use will continue to assert meanwhile its long-remembered virtues."

Egyptian jasper has a brownish outward tinge, shading to a paler hue internally. Found on the shores of the Red Sea, it was greatly used by the ancient Egyptians in the making and engraving of seals and amulets. The Chaldaeans also employed red and green jasper for their seals, to which they seem to have attached a mystic importance. Every person of consequence possessed one, worn hanging from the neck or wrist, and which he never willingly parted with during life. At his death his seal was buried with him, in order that no improper use might ever be made of it. In the making of their engraved "sigilla" blood-stones were much used by the old Gnostics, whose faith in the magic virtue of these mysterious seals formed part of their religious beliefs, "the sacred operations and mysteries of seals" that Cornelius Agrippa writes of. And there is no doubt that many of these traditions concerning the hidden virtues of gems, preserved throughout the Dark Ages by a few learned men, eventually found their way to Europe and so into mediaeval teachings, by means of the increased intercourse with Oriental nations brought about by the Crusades.

Blood-stones were used in ancient forms of incantations, and moreover were said to be powerful amulets against the Evil Eye. They also rendered their wearers invisible, and preserved friendship between men. But, say the old authorities, for friendship between man and woman emeralds should be worn; and in the case of two women, let each wear a turquoise, thereby securing a faithful friend. Emeralds were believed to strengthen the memory, for which purpose Culpepper (1656), amongst some mineral prescriptions added to his famous *Herbal,* advises their being worn in a ring.

Washington Irving, in his *Conquest of Granada,* tells of a wonderful emerald so large that a table was made of it, which Taric, the Arab chief, looted from the city of Medina Celi in the days when the Arab inroads into Spain began. This marvelous jewel had originally formed part of the spoil taken at Rome by Alaric, when the sacred city was sacked by the Goths. "It possessed talismanic powers ; for tradition affirms that it was the work of genii, and had been wrought by them for King Solomon the Wise." According to Arab legends this table was a mirror revealing all great events, "insomuch that by looking on it the possessor might behold battles and sieges, and feats of chivalry, and all actions worthy of renown."

A seventeenth century writer tells us gravely about the topaz, "If you put it into boiling water, it doth so cool it, that you may presently put your hands into it without harm." Regarding this stone, an extremely gifted "crystal-gazer" (who is an old acquaintance of the writer) says, "Anyone who has lost a high position and desires to regain it, should never be without a topaz." The same person declares that clients who come for advice, always appear to her in certain lights of varying colors, and that this "aura" (combined with the knowledge of the inquirer's planetary influences) enables her to tell him what precious stone will bring him good fortune. She also advises no one to wear a *single* pearl, "It is very bad luck." Some people say that a bride should not wear pearls, for they are emblematic of tears. Yet the old "dream-books" tell us that to dream of these gems, "of purest ray serene," is lucky! But there is one historical dream that contradicts this idea. We read that the night before Henry the Fourth of France was assassinated by Ravaillac, his Queen dreamed very vividly that her diamonds in her crown were turned to pearls—significant of grief—and in the murder of her Royal husband the Queen saw the too real interpretation of her dream. The Dowager Queen Margarita of Italy, who possesses pearls renowned for splendor, had also to suffer the terrible shock of a husband's death by assassination.

Most traditions affirm that the diamond inspires its wearer with courage, and gives protection against enemies. Yet one old writer says of this stone, "It is reported to make him that bears it unfortunate." Which seems to have been the experience of the ill-fated Mary, Queen of Scots; for the diamond ring given her by Ruthven, as a talisman against her enemies, certainly failed in its effect most grievously. To dream of diamonds portends gossip, and "if you see them sparkle and do not touch them, it foretells return of happiness." While to dream of a garnet means future wealth!

Of comparatively modern origin is the idea that opals bring bad luck to their possessors. In old times these glorious gems were much esteemed as having potent virtue against all diseases of the eyes; and it is said that in ancient Mexico the opal was considered a sacred stone, containing an essence of the divine fire which created the world. Russians are particularly superstitious on the subject of opals, regarding their influence as fatal, and calling them the embodiment of the Evil Eye. Few people in fact have a good word to say for this beautiful and mysterious jewel, and on all sides, one is told that only those born in October should wear it, in which case it brings good fortune. Otherwise "it is fatal to love, and will break friend ship." Everyone knows the story of the famous Spanish opal ring, which was given to Alfonso the Thirteenth by the Comtesse de Castiglione, who bore a grudge against the King, for some fancied slight. Possessed in turn by several of the Royal family, this ring is said to have brought death to six of them, till at last, after the death of Alfonso himself, Queen Christina took the fatal jewel and had it hung round the neck of the Virgin of Almudena, the patron saint of Madrid.

In a letter to the writer, a friend says, "A relation told me once of an opal that a man she knew wore in a ring; and it belonged originally to the eye of an Indian idol. He said it had brought death or misfortune in some form to anyone to whom he had given it. Several people coveting the stone had taken it on chance, but he always had it returned before twelve months were out." Another friend writes, "We have a ring in our family which I consider most unlucky; it is set with emeralds and opals, and was the engagement ring of her grandmother. The engagement lasted seven years on account of unexpected obstacles, and when the marriage took place, the bridegroom died six months afterwards, and his wife be came a permanent invalid. She left the ring to a relative, but I have always begged her not to wear it." Apropos of the idea that opals are fatal to friendship, the following instance (which though slight is interesting) is contributed by a correspondent: "I know a Mrs. Z- who had an opal brooch given her by a great friend. Having a 'feeling' about opals, she did not want to take the gift, but ended by doing so. From the time she began to wear it, her friend's affection seemed to cool and gradually they drifted apart, though with no apparent reason. This upset Mrs. Z- very much, and she felt sure the opal was to blame. Without telling her friend, she gave the brooch to a person whose 'lucky-stone' it happened to be, and from that day she regained the friendship that she feared was lost."

One sometimes hears of jewels other than opals, which seem to bring a curse on all who possess them. The famous Koh-i-noor diamond has this reputation, its career being a very checkered one until it came to England fifty years ago, since when —happily— its evil spirit seems to have slumbered. But the writer is reminded of a story which is a good illustration of a "cursed jewel." A certain Miss Seward, who was a sceptic regarding occult phenomena, had a friend Mrs. H- , who one day begged Miss Seward to go with her to a clairvoyant, saying,

"I am sure he will convert you; he will answer any question you wish, and if you are ill, he will tell you what ails you, even if your doctors don't know." Feeling rather curious after this description, Miss Seward consented to visit the clairvoyant, and as a test took with her a glove belonging to another person, a young girl of sixteen. This girl had been ill more or less for some time; without having any particular malady that could be diagnosed, she was never well. Miss Seward gave the glove to the clairvoyant, who held it, and presently said, "This is not your glove; it belongs to quite a young girl. She is always ill, and she will never be well as long as she wears that amulet round her neck. It is the price of blood. I don't say she must throw it away, but she must never wear it, and if possible, never be in the same room with it." Miss Seward did not know that her friend wore anything in the nature of an amulet, but full of excitement after the clairvoyant's communication, she hastened to see her, and, as frequently happened, found her in bed. After some casual conversation, Miss Seward asked, "By the way, do you ever wear any sort of necklace or chain round your neck?" "Oh yes," was the reply, "I always wear this old necklace; it is an heirloom, and my father thinks so much of it, that I wear it to keep it safely." Miss Seward then told her friend what the clairvoyant had said, and easily persuaded her to remove the necklace, and have it put away in a never-used attic. Almost immediately the invalid began to feel better, and in ten days she was quite well. Her father when told was greatly interested in the clairvoyant's assertion, and set to work making inquiries respecting the past history of the necklace, with the result that he discovered it had been connected with *two murders* in Paris!

The historical stone known as the "Blue Diamond" has just returned to France, from which country it was brought to England towards the close of the eighteenth century. Some years later it became the property of a banker named Hope. When he died, he left it to his family, but several of his heirs having died in some tragic manner, one after the other, the remaining ones, attributing these misfortunes to the possession of the diamond, became alarmed and determined to be rid of the jewel. So, it was sold and taken to America, where it remained for a great many years, until quite lately its owner parted with it to a French bidder, for the sum—it is said—of two million francs.

Though not strictly coming under the category of "precious stones," yet in interest the crystal ranks above many of its more valuable brethren. With its absolute purity and clearness, and its delightful coolness to the touch, it is no wonder that the ancients ascribed marvelous powers to this beautiful form of quartz. The art of divination by the crystal is older than man's knowledge; while today it is said that the Japanese practice it in order to "commune with the Deity, by gazing long and intently on a large globe of pure crystal placed in the center of the room. . . . The answer to their petitions comes through the crystal." It was formerly believed that the crystal sphere itself, by virtue of its "magnetic properties," was accountable for the prophetic pictures and visions produced in its clear depths. But most people have now come to understand that it is the seer himself who elicits the visions, and that to persons gifted with that particular psychic sense, it is a matter of indifference what they "gaze" at, so long as it is a help to concentration of attention. Other stones were often used for the purpose, particularly, says Dr. Fernie, the "pale water-green beryl, or delicate aquamarine; this water-green being astrologically considered as a color especially under the influence of the moon, an orb exerting very great magnetic influence." It is true that professional "crystal-gazers" sometimes tell their clients to hold the crystal ball for several minutes, alleging that the stone is thereby influenced in some way by the personality of the inquirer. But it is doubtful whether this part of the performance is in the least necessary in the case of a genuine seer, though to the uninitiated such a preliminary makes the whole business more impressive.

Some years ago, when travelling abroad, the writer met a Mr. X-, a civil engineer, who in the exercise of his profession had passed much of his life in Egypt. One evening when the conversation had turned on "fortune-telling" and kindred subjects, and different experiences were being exchanged, Mr. X- related the following story, which he said was to him as inexplicable as it was true: "By the side of a road close to Cairo, an Egyptian boy sits all day with a crystal ball, from which he professes to be able to read the future. One day my friend Arnold and I were walking past this boy, when Arnold stopped and said, 'Look here, let's have our fortunes told.' I said, 'Nonsense!' and wanted to go on. But Arnold was determined, so he gave the boy a coin, and jokingly told him to look into the crystal. The boy was silent for some time, then said, 'I see a room, but it is not like our rooms.' He then described what sounded like an English bedroom. Arnold said, 'Yes. Go on. What else do you see?' After a while, still looking intently at the ball, the boy answered, 'I see a woman lying on a couch. She is old, but she looks like you. She is dying.' He would say no more, and put down the crystal. We walked on, Arnold seeming preoccupied and depressed. I said, 'Surely you did not believe that nonsense?' He replied that he could not help thinking it strange, because the boy had actually most accurately described his mother's room in England! However, we began to talk of other things, and personally I thought no more of the matter, until a few days later I was shocked to hear that Arnold had received news of his mother's death, which had unexpectedly taken place on the day that the boy saw the vision in the crystal."

Although it is rather a digression from the subject of this article, the writer is tempted to conclude with a short story

174

which she thinks illustrative of the assertion, that it is really no occult property of a crystal, in itself, that produces the vision, but that other objects able to give an effect of depth and repose, answer a real clairvoyant's purpose equally well. In the words of the narrator, "My mother and I were staying with my godmother Miss Power, who lives in a little country village in Blankshire. One evening after dinner we were talking about crystal-gazing, etc., and she said that she often saw visions in an *ordinary plain tumbler* filled with water. We asked her to try then, and she proceeded to do so. After describing one or two scenes . . . which we could not identify, she suddenly exclaimed that she saw several war-ships and a number of fishing-boats enveloped in clouds of smoke, one of which appeared to be sinking, and on board which men were rushing to and fro in a terrified condition. We couldn't imagine what this could be, but on opening the papers next morning, the first thing we saw was the account of the 'Dogger Bank' incident, when the Russian war-ships fired on the English fishing-fleet. I'm sorry to say we can't remember the exact date, but of course any book dealing with the war would give it to you. Miss Power saw the vision late on Sunday evening, and being right in the country, there was no chance of her having seen any rumor of the affair in a Sunday paper, as one might be inclined to suspect in the case of someone living in town. We always thought it rather an extra ordinary story, and one of the strangest points about it is that my godmother is one of the most matter of fact people it is possible to imagine . . . altogether the very last woman one would think likely to be gifted with 'occult powers' of any description."

Faerie Ireland

by Lady Archibald Campbell

On Hallow-e'en in braw moonlight
The faerie hosts they ride
Through England, Scotland, Ireland,
Through all the world wide.
                                    —Old Ballad.

Ireland is a psychic country. The Irish people are pre eminently sensitive to the psychic influences of Nature. Figuratively speaking, they have touched the far-away Island of Beauty. All inspiring causes have led to this result.

The Celts are by inheritance mystics; they are magicians. Their initiation is above all the knowledge and power of the soul; love of beauty is their means of initiation. They have laid hold of the belief that in ancient times God was the primeval incident out of which first came the Celt.

In Scotland, the heroic past is told as a song that is forgotten, instead of an eternal cause of fame; whereas the Irish Celts have kept in touch with their deified ancestors, affirming that they still draw near to the border and are their friends.

We are but human caterpillars— fumblers, without breadth of knowledge, until we learn the adamantine strength of that force called psychic, and how to use it. When we have realized its potency, we shall have realized the ancient idea that human force and valor were inseparably associated with this power, and depended on the knowledge of how to wield it in war, and direct it in the cause of peace. The modem warrior has trampled on it, crushed it, and has thus robbed himself of a strength latent within him. For it was a cult which made of our ancestors, invulnerable heroes, and the only cult by which we can come in touch with the heroic past we have so long set aside.

It is a matter of history that nowhere except in Gaeldom could there be found such pregnant perpetuity of the ancient beliefs. The armies of the mighty "Shee" signify to the Irish the spirits of the ancient races, including the Divine race of the Tutha Dea Danaan— the tribes of the Goddess Dina, who held sovereignty of Great Ireland prior to the arrival of the sons of Mil, by whom they were dispossessed of earthly sway— mighty mystics, magicians, spiritualists, under standing the formative power of Nature, the principle of Life, the power which contains the essence of life and character in everything, "The Azoth or creative principle, the Mysterium Magnum." "Everything being of a threefold nature," said Paracelsus, "there is a threefold aspect of Alchemy"; the science of modem Chemistry deals only with the lowest aspects of it. We Gaels, it is said, inherit our mysticism from them, the Danaans, that mortal immortal race who, it is supposed, never saw death. To group or grade the hidden clans of spirit Irelands, glens and mountains, is impossible. The parts assigned to them in Irish mystical romance were especially that of protectors, fosterers, inspirers of vegetable and animal life. In short, their dominion was over all forces in Nature. To interpret something of Nature magic we have to go back to the runes. In the wandering annals of sweet "Faerie," in Scotland as in Ireland, spirits of the ancient Celtic races are identified as the Deathless Folk or Lasting People; in the West Highlands as the Secret or Hidden People— Races great and small; People of Safety or Men of Peace. In the Wonderland of the hollow hills everywhere in Gaeldom their dwellings have been located, and oversea in Tir nan Oge— the land of the ever young.

It is traditional that they visibly controlled the cereals and pasture, until they were offended for some reason and ceased. Have they ceased? According to the evidence of our inner senses, of hearing and of seeing, they are still revealed through Life's processes, forever moving more and more wonderfully on, having made the flooring of their world everywhere, working through, permeating all Nature. We should on bended knees fall upon the grass and give thanks to them for every blade that grows. When we see patient toilers living by the spade, sowing to reap and gathering in abundantly, their few acres have been blessed by the goodwill and shadowy hands of the passing multitude. My eyes have been opened to see that many spirits do pass by astray from man's interests, but not all. We recognize among these clans of passing people a "stewardie." Out of the twilight they are coming over, drawing closer to humanity, and in fellowship with us are evolving with us, in our cycle. Seeing that through human consciousness we retain the human element of Faerie, we must see them, they are floating round us, our senses are in their atmosphere. It may be that as we environ the power called psychic, so shall we environ Nature as they do, and control the vital principle which pervades all things.

The fact is, that the grand ancient naturalistic mythology which Ireland shares with Vedic India, lost hold of the peasant mind only when the understanding and the mutual sympathy existing between themselves and the spirits of their heroic ancestors had been disturbed, crossed, by mistaken saints who, in monopolizing the right of intercourse with the transcendental worlds, prejudiced the people against those whom they had regarded as their benefactors and gods of the earth's progress. Fear begets fear and estrangement. The power of those Lords of Life and Increase was impeded. The primitive Christian reformers, who robbed hostile forces of their powers for evil, must have equally robbed the powers beneficent to work unseen through Nature's forces, directing them for the general good. Already, before the advent of Saint Columba from Ireland, the Druids in Scotland had worked for harm in worshipping through the Great Mystery of Nature nothing but the living powers of ill. The flying angel hosts of Saint Columba's visions in 565 A.D. were the faery hosts of the Pagan seers.

I am staying in a house known as The Wonderful Barn. It was once a fine castell before it was bombarded by the Danes. The venerable farmer, my host, with a prodigious memory, has not been without psychic experiences. Here is one he told me, "When Christians and cattle were standing knee-deep in water, just before the terrible famine of 1846, I aroused one night every person in the house from their beds to see the portent— for portent it surely was— slowly passing across the heavens. Three hours we watched it— three moons and through them a flaming cross."

In the courtyard of this Wonderful Barn I have watched the building of the great corn-stacks, higher and higher; "the squirrel's granary is full and the harvest's done." In such a place the Provencal legend of "La Belle Dame sans Merci," and other spell bound knights, the enthralment of Thomas the Rhymer and the tale of "The Yonge Tam Lin" stolen to "Faerie," come to mind, as true events which, having happened elsewhere, might happen here any day, because the Passing People are about. The sweep of their hills is at the back of the house. Over them, like rolling mists, their pageants pass. The yet seen mighty hosts of Shee, led by their Queens, float by with hearts of flame and wings of star dust, or whirl by on horseback dressed in the twelve colors of the winds, or mantled but by their tossing hair, their radiating aureoles and colored emanations differentiating their character and qualities of mind.

180

Sometimes of human stature, sometimes Titanic, as the Eastern gods and goddesses of whom the poet wrote, " on their vast faces mystery and dreams." In Gaeldom it is said "The Shee ride the winds." Do they direct them? Do they direct that wind which brings fulfilment of long hopes but to carry them away? Everything blows one thing towards another. Comes Fate — feeling its way like the kiss of the wind. Anything one may turn into ridicule but Fate. It is too solemn, too infinitely great. The fateful wind which wafts the kiss from the lips of unknown lover to unknown lover, bears the pollen from stigma to stigma of appointed flowers; and in the wind, and like the wind, infatuate as love, deep and impetuous—mysterious and as changeful— come and go the Passing People.

This morning when the blackbird flew up there, the corncrake craked among the corn riggs which stand out like molten gold touched by the rising sun. These are the faerie acres— "the twenty and one." The glen is called a *gentle* glen because haunted by the Passing People. There are tongues of genius every where. Especially here in this faerie center tongues of genius have found utterance on earth. Echoes from the Great Invisible have been caught by men, two men of whom Ireland is justly proud, milking them more than mystic poets— great seers. When I went up this morning to the faerie pasture where that blackbird flew, I looked down on the city far below, lying half lost in a shroud of its own smoke. A sullen storm cloud hung above the sea, but the billowy acres where I was shone emerald green, splashed by beams of breaking light as from the other world. I heard a distant convent bell, the tinkle of sheep bells, the lowing cattle, the laughter of the glittering little diamond river twisting down the gentle glen past the Peacock Well of Healing, which lies in a deep hollow on the hillside, and blown across my ears the notes of a horn.

Over the circling hills, covered with heather, fern and gorse, the Deathless, the Lasting, or Passing People have right of way. They are lords over rivers and seas. In the heart of a hill a Smith sits at a forge. At every stroke of his anvil fly the sparks. When asked what he does there, he answers, "I am forging souls."

The light was streaking on a low thatched roof, towards which I made my way. An old blind man lives here, and here I am always in and out. This cabin faces the twenty-one acres and the little diamond river. Round the door those yellow flowers are growing in quantities, called by the Irish folk the faerie's boholon— the horses of the Little Good People, on which, according to tradition, they first rode over from Erin to Alba. The paths over the hills are as numerous as the stories the blind man tells about them. The one I liked best was about a Leprechaun and how he caught it at the Peacock's Well. The learned in faerie lore know that the ancient race of the Leprechaun has ever been associated with luck by the poor, for it is he who knows where the crocks of gold are hid. Leprechaun is a corruption from the original name "Luchorpan," which signifies a wee or little body, about six inches high. The blind man was sitting in the chimney nook when I came in. I lost no time in telling him I came to hear how he caught the faery. "Och," he said, "it is a long day since I caught the leprechaun. I was young and souple then." He pointed up the hill to the Peacock Well.

"Sure, it will be going on for thirty years or more that I was up at the Well of Healing— they call it the Peacock's Well— when of a sudden out of a thorn bush leapt a little red-capped fellow, the smallest little lad I ever saw in my life, not two foot high. 'In God's name,' I cried, 'who are you?' He turned and ran. I took up and after him, over hill and rock and dell and down, till at last I fell on him, caught him in a furze

182

bush, and in my arms, I brought him home. His hair was reddish, his skin very clear but dark in color. A little red cap fitted neat upon his head. His dress was green, soft to the touch, shorter than a kilt; his boots were as soft as moss over his naked legs. I gripped him close in my arms and took him home. I called to the woman to look at what I had got. 'What doll is it you have there?' she cried. 'A living one,' I said, and put it on the dresser. We feared to lose it; we kept the door locked. It talked and muttered to itself queer words. Not one word we could understand. At times it would smile as though it had knowledge of what we were saying. It might have been near on a fortnight since we had the faery, when I said to the woman, 'Sure, if we show it in the great city we will be made up.' Now this was much on our minds. So, we put it in a cage. At night we would leave the cage door open, and we would hear it stirring through the house. When we struck a match, it would jump on to the dresser. We fed it on bread and rice and milk out of a cup at the end of a spoon. It would take nothing from the woman, but when she put the cup beside it, and no one looked, some way the food was taken, the cup left empty. It might have been a fortnight less or more when again I went to the Peacock's Well for a drink. Out of a bush there jumped a wee one, if anything smaller than the one we had. Bedad! they are souple the faeries. It ran, and I ran. Souple as I was then that one was too souple for me. I ran till I was like to drop. I lost it. When I won home, I said to the woman, 'I am all in a swither.' The sweat was pouring from me. 'I have lost another, at the Peacock's Well, like the first,' I said, pointing to the little one on the dresser, sitting with eyes fixed on me. He sprang up with a scream. 'Geoffray, O Wee, looking for me'; and with a spring he was out of the door and away through the darkness. Some years after my son, at that time unborn, was playing in the shed among the leaves, sudden he raised a cry, 'Mother, mother, come and see a wee red-capped bit of a mannie, leaping out of the leaves. He is sitting on the top of the wall.' On the minute we stirred up every stick and leaf, but whatever way it was the mannie was gone. The woman took up the word and said 'Och, och, we lost our luck when we lost the leprechaun.'"

"I have heard," I said, "that even to talk of taking a faery is to make the hate of faeries come upon you." The blind man answered sadly, "For me, though I've lost my sight, the day I took the leprechaun I thought no harm, only that we would be made up. I am thinking different now by the way things have gone. Sure, we are among them in God's world who are born to be poor." He continued, "There was one, Mike Mulligan, who was always dreaming if he was on London Bridge he would be made up. There he went. And for three days on London Bridge he walked. It was on the third evening a little red-capped mannie dressed in green came to him, and said, 'Is there any harm asking you what makes you walk up and down here these three days?' 'No harm at all in life,' said the man. 'I was always dreaming that if I was on London Bridge I would be made up,' and the wee mannie with the red cap said, 'I was dreaming that if I was back in Ireland at the back of Mike Mulligan's house, I would dig up two crocks of gold.' Then in a whiff the mannie went.

"Mike turned. The words of the red-capped mannie on the tip of his tongue he kept to himself. Home he went. He dug and dug till deep in the earth he won at the back of his house two crocks of gold, and a rich man he was to the end of his days. Where you see the rainbow start, dig there, and there you'll find a crock of gold. When I was young and souple, I can mind the day I had the rainbow end many a time about me on the hill, but I lost my chances.

"One evening up there," he said, pointing towards a "rathin" where stands a ruin, "no ruin was there, but a fine house of light, and out at the door came many young people,

184

dancing the clap hands dance, and making music and much fun. They called me by my name, and circled round me, and drew me after them into the house; I danced with them, how long I cannot tell. I slipped out by the door; I fell asleep, and when I woke, there was the ruin as you see it, and none there beside me but old Kate, one I know well, milking a goat. Another day close to the giant's grave I was, standing with a heavy burden of sticks upon my back, when all at once I saw beside me a wee wee woman, two foot high, dressed in black. The wrinkles on her face were wonderful. She was looking at the bottom of the deep glen where the waterfall was rushing. 'Gomorrah,' I said, 'what are you?' She made no answer. 'By God,' I said, 'what would you here?' She said, 'I'd take that load of yours, an it were twice as strong.' Of the meaning I have not the knowledge. She said it twice and disappeared. Now, lady, will you not be thinking with all this, that somewhere hid there will be— might be wee folk of this earth, that are as real as you or me?" I said, "Not in Ireland. No such race could be about those hills without being discovered. They cannot belong to our sphere."

It was a lovely evening when last I saw him sitting at his door. Across the glen came the echo of a horn, clear but faint. I had often heard it. He said: "Lady, do you hear that ? . . . I often hear it, and their happy voices too. It is the hour they will be gathering yonder at the ruined gate, before they ride across the world. . . . The Lord protect you and prolong your days." As I looked back at him who knew not night from day, helpless, sitting in the growing darkness . . . I could but wish he might get back his faery.

A few years now have passed since Lady Alix Egerton and Miss Coleman Smith visited this gentle glen. They made straight for the little river, bordered by the heathery hill on one side and upon the other by the tangled brushwood and the broken ground beyond. A fair wind blew that afternoon, and

185

before they reached the little ford, a certain group of stones mid-stream, they heard a sound— a coming wave of music. Was it the wind? We know there is a slogan in the sound of wind. They maintain it was not wind nor sound of wind, but a journeying music which met them, now fast, now slow, a burden that had no beginning nor yet an end. They reached the ford, and on the rock mid-stream sat down. The eddying gusts swept by, the coming music stayed, becoming more and more distinct. Presently the rock began to stir, it breathed as if in sleep; it seemed to palpitate as if alive. They both felt this; they touched it. It was cold; though cold to touch, directly they raised their hands, a hot air struck their palms. Then slowly, silently the near rock moved aside, and left a reft where hitherto there had been none; then slowly, silently, moved back again to its place. Keeping the center of the wind, though lost in part, they heard the clear definite beat of a march played upon stringed instruments— harps, violins, reed-pipes, strike of cymbals, beat of drums, with much singing, calling of voices, and the clash of arms. The music was loud, so loud as to be almost deafening, louder than the fretful gusts, and independent of the wind's direction, as from a vast advancing throng, who, all unseen, had now surrounded them. Upon the right hand of the diamond river, on the hillside, riders galloped on white horses, and their cloaks, blue, green and grey, streamed in the wind, as in bounding stride their horses rose from earth commanding earth and air. Across the broken ground upon the left marched ranks on foot. Close by, and looking down on them, Lady Alix saw a tall man wrapped in a blue cloak; he leaned on a cross-hilted sword. Nearer still huddled together, were three old men like sages; a young man talked with them; his hair was red, his dress was blue; and as they faded out a queenly woman crossed the little river, arrayed in blue, wearing a crown of prehistoric shape. She vanished as down upon the surface of the stream skimmed a salmon wearing on its head a silver crown.

186

There is a local tradition which relates that Finn McCoul, the famous hunter, warrior, and chief, caught the Salmon of Knowledge in a pool upon the Boyne, which is below Slane Hill. Of this ancient symbol my friends had never heard.

We may ask, and ask in vain, why apparently certain places, to the exclusion of others, are centers of psychic forces— forces which may as appropriately be termed human forces, life forces. For they are in the air we breathe and known to the Seer who sees the sea and land beyond the Sea of seas. All we know is that such forces filling the Nature-world are liberated by Her which neither physicists nor psychologists can weigh, measure, or manipulate. We might as well attempt to weigh the imponderable as try to define why certain localities are so permeated with secret virtues, so charged with indeterminate influences or emanations that one who is exceptionally sensitive passes under their power and becomes prescient. It is for the student of the occult to go further into the beyond and discover whether certain areas favored by the hosts become charged with the quickening force of their wills, impregnated with the magnetism, the very essence of their presence.

Where the rocks are abused with sound of tom-tom, their mountains amazed by tumult of trams and trains, the ancient names defaced by strangers, Slieve Trim in County Tyrone familiarized into Bessie Bell, a sister mountain vulgarized into Louisa Gray, it is not wonderful that races, great and small, retire further within the Great Within, there to enjoy invisibility inviolate. Yet it was in County Tyrone I went up to see old Robin and his wife. He was at the back of the house, cutting the rushes for the hogs' beds. The wife, dusting a chair with her apron, invited me with "Come beside the fire and sit." I said, "Will you tell me about the Little People?" "Och, och, aye, the Lord be yet our help. It's the faeries you will be asking for, and it's the truth I will be telling you, and no lies, with the God Himself listening. It will be years since I saw the leprechaun, when I was a girl away in Donegal. It was Good Friday, when the other girls were after the oysters and mussels for the feast on Easter Day, on the shore at Swilly Bay, and I stopped at the owld Proosh Bridge. Says I to myself, 'I'll hide under the brig and call cuck-oo at them when they pass back.' Sudden before me stood a wee wee man, two-foot high— if he was that— a dainty wee man with a red cap on his head and green coat and leggings upon him. No bigger but what he would walk upright beneath the chair, there where you sit. 'What fetched you here?' he cried. 'To call cuck-oo,' I said. He spoke angrily, 'Be off with ye; if ever you come back again I'll ban ye.' I did not give him time to say another word. I made for home as fast as 1 could run."

I am now in Sligo, where to the seer the spaces of land, sea, and mountain vibrate, filled with the breath of gods, permeated through and through with forces from the very arteries of the Eternal God. Over the rocks where I am sitting, above the bay of shining sand, between the going down of the sun and the rising of the moon, night is falling like a veil, to the same rainbow-music of sea and land and sound of rippling laughter, which Ireland's greatest seer must have heard a few years since, when his eyes were opened, and he saw and painted from this very place three women of the Shee stealing for love a human child. The sleepy foam is curving over the sand as on that evening of glamour, when out of it, clothed but with their mantling hair and rays of star dust attracting them to the Godhead from which they came, these three gracious faerie women stepped to meet the wretched boy in tatters, who waded out of the crest of a wave with awe and wonder in his steps in answer to their persuasive words and beckoning call.

"Come away, oh human child:

To the waters and the wild,

With a faery, hand in hand,

For the world's more full of weeping than you can understand."

If the love of truth transparent is displayed in all heavenly art, glory of wings must be in form, in harmony of outline, in texture, and in structure, to picture motion, and symbolize flight. Surely our wings shall be put on or off at will, as fleet Mercury put on or off winged anklets, jovial Bacchus his horns. The immortal women of this vision, wingless and undraped, cloaked in their spreading hair, trip their errand with light. From the "genteel" angel of convention they are far removed, as far as light from darkness, as beauty from ugliness, as truth is from a lie— having no kinship to those beings bristling with quills, sexless, yet draped to satisfy smug respectability. In the poise of their tenuous, ethereal bodies, the sway of their uncertain steps over the silver sands, we see abstraction, aloofness—we see in that mystic impression what the seer-painter saw and knew: they are wandering in the twilight of Eternity.

A little further from the scene of the vision, I came upon the "Splash or Flash of the Lapwing" — a small inland loch— where on the hillock above, the same seer saw and painted a woman of the "Shee" standing, fluttering in a rainbow-hued kirtle, blowing on a triton's horn. When I passed the Splash today it lay in shadow; there was a noise of whispering reeds and rushing wings — lapwings, flashing through them, playing hide and seek. I grieved no Shee were there.

In my hill wanderings further west, over the faerie bogs— bogs which are fonts in the spirit hills of the Passing People— I came upon a low thatched roof. Within the cabin a very old bed ridden man was dying, of four score years and ten. He was alone. I spoke to him, he never moved or answered, his eyes were open wide, and with a vacant stare.

"He is far through," said the woman who came in, " he's just for making his peace with his Maker."

At that he smiled and said to me, "You are a stranger."

His skin was dark as a Spaniard's. I talked of the wonder I found in Ireland and said, "I am a Celt like yourself."

He looked pleased, but when I edged on to faery lore, he muttered, "As many as were seeing them in the days gone by are seeing them no more."

I said, "But some Hielanders have the two sights complete."

He answered dreamily, "The day was when *I* had the sight for them."

I said, "Tell me of that."

He shook his head. "I cannot mind them now; I might tell you how the Milesians came to Ireland. I would tell it clearer in the Gaelic, but will try it in the English. The day was, when I was a scholar. Something yet of a scholar I am." He raised himself with effort, and half sitting, supporting his frail body on his nervy arms and hands, with much dramatic power, as if the legendary past stood present before his eyes, began this Son of Milith:. . .

"In the days of old sailing over the wide seas came a prince, son of him then King of Spain. The course that galley took was as the winds favored it, and the fortune of that

190

beautiful prince. But for all their travel neither he nor any man of all his crew had yet won sight of land. Now came to them the sound of breakers, still they saw no land, for thickening mists hung all around. In Ireland at that time King Ganlon ruled, wise in magic. His watchers on the heights had viewed the coming of the ship and warned the King; powerful in spell, he girded Ireland with the magic fog. The world was closed— before them and behind them. The Prince bethought him now to turn the prow and once again put out to sea, when through that wall of darkness came unto his ears a sound, the humming of a bee, stirring the foggy air round and about him. 'Land is here!' he cried; they dropped the anchor. Led by the humming of the bee the Prince landed—crossed a fair white strand where sat upon a rock a maiden singing, combing her hair. She turned her face away from him. He asked her who she was. She answered warily, like at the corner of her mouth, 'I am the daughter of King Ganlon, King of Eire.' Then said the Prince, 'I am the son of him who now is King of far Espana'; she answered never a word. 'Turn round,' he said; and she would not. Again he spoke: 'Turn, thou whose face divined is the torchlight of my dreams.' Then turned the lovely maid, arose and standing on her feet looked down on him between her half-shut lids. Then fell the Prince, and lowly at her feet prayed her to go with him; but she would not. Thus spake he, 'Whatsoever a King your father be, let it be known to him, you I would win, will wed you and none other.' Softly she laughed and through her falling hair she spoke, enchantress that she was, 'How long?' . . . And he looked round at Eire, searching for a measure wherewithal to weigh the burden of his love. . . . 'As long as. . .' But the humming of the wise bumbee had ceased. The crafty maid had cast the spell of silence over Eire the better now to hear the beating of his heart. Now came a sounding wave upon the rock. . . . 'As long as sea shall dash on rocks and till the sun goes off the firmament forever.' Quoth the Maid, 'I will unto the King my father and return again.' Swift as a doe to him she sped, and thus she spake: 'Behold a mighty stranger faring over seas, son of a King, has landed and declared his love. He swears by might of Eire that he will wed me and none other!' Then spake with scorn, the King, 'Call out my watchers. Make known to this rash stranger that I fight in air, on land and sea.' She laughed unto herself. And to the rocks unseen she fled. Because of her enchantments even the watchers slept. Thus spake she to the Prince, 'Take this, my father's word, "I fight in air, on land and sea."' With joy the Prince made answer, 'So be it! Him will I fight, in air, on land and sea.' With eyes bent on the ground unto the magic King she went again, casting on him her witch's spell— volition. 'This wretched stranger cannot fight in air, nor yet on land or sea, and yet will not begone. Were it not well my Father King shall choose the way he shall be slain?' Up rose King Ganlon in his wrath: 'Verily a weakling or a fool. I slay him on the sea!' The witch maid laughed behind her hair and ran to him she loved, foreseeing to the end, whispered within his ear the secret that the wise bumbee knew well. Made answer that bold Prince, 'I fight the King on sea.' Sang the uplifted maid and hum-m-ed the secret bee 'Great Manaan be with us.' . . . So met and fought King Ganlon and the Prince of Far Espana, and he it was who slew the King, and thus the race of Milith came to Ireland."

A small example this of how strong are the links of the great psychic chain which connects the Celtic race with their ancestors.

In Highland mythology god Michael is spoken of as the god of mountains and seas—Michael of the White Steeds, Michael the Victorious. The Arya tongue has given us Michael the Archangel, Bearer of the Sword of Light, and Guardian of the Cup, dwelling among the hosts of the Watchers. The Celtic tongue has given another name to "the rider of the glistening horses with the glaive of Light"—a name euphonious as the

192

sound of the sea —Manaan— Great Manaan. Although there is no suggestion that Manaan and Michael are the same in Celtic literature, an authority points out that the similarity of both Michael in the Semitic and Manaan in the Celtic suggest their original identity.

Achill —the Island of Achill— in the extreme north-west of Ireland, is under the protection of Croghan Mountain. It is pronounced Crohan. Like the other Irish mountains, Croghan is under the Ray of Great Manaan. Manaan appeared in many forms to the heroes— he is said to appear as an old man to the poor and to speak words of wisdom to them, and give to them prophetic gifts whose lives are linked to their country.

Achill aspirated softly —as it should be— by the Gaelic tongue, is like the sighs and echo of the sighs we hear all round the island from winds and waves. At the foot of Crohan where I write, wild Nature's sobs are blent with the subdued laments of the very, very poorest of humanity, who, in piteous want and decrepit old age, seem to live but a life in death. This is only the negative side. For Crohan is a small firm out of the Great Spiritual Whole. Through all and everything there is a noise of the lapping tide upon the spheres, and over the dredging sands of time. If it were not for this, one must fall under the burden of a great sadness and believe that the island is haunted by spirit clans unmindful of their trust.

A storm is raging round the fisherman's hut where I am lodged. With shrieks and hoarse exasperated howls the wind protests, batters at the windows, opens shaky doors, tears at the roof until the house from floor to rafter quakes and reels. The sudden lulls so ominous between each frantic cannonade that one feels the next must be the last before the walls shall fall.

Oh, still the night, the dark, dark wave, oh come.

Great Manaan I still the night. . .

At last comes daybreak. Lashed to spume, the sea is playing a witch's harmony round the cabin door and against the giant rock battlements of Achill thousands of feet high. Between the squalls I have crept down among the rocks, where a knot of men, women and children from their hovels have crawled out, and propped half nude against their tottering walls, listen to the wail of one who in losing his cranky curragh from the shore has lost his all. An old woman like a walnut, riddled with wrinkles, carries on her back an infant screaming itself hoarse. She said: "It is blind the crater will be for life— it's a month gone that its eyes are closed with the sand in them. It takes on like that all night, all day." A priest comes by and lays his finger on the swollen lids of the child, mutters a prayer, signs them with the cross. The eyes open, and the woman cries, "Bless the Lord."

The old Irish people still chant runes in the name of the ancient gods. They are chanted as the hand is laid on the head of the afflicted. They have bone-setting runes, blood-stopping runes, in words which have been handed down from generation to generation. Eye-witnesses to this day testify to their efficacy.

While I am watching the fleeing spindrift— the riven scarfs of the fleeting storm spinners, the oldest fisherman in this poor village, in the shelter of his cabin door, tells me how he saw "Tir nan Ogue," the Land of the Ever Young, "more clearly than you ever see Clare Island from the shore upon the clearest day. I was at the deep-sea fishing," he said, "when suddenly it rose before me. Great white cliffs were there. So near I was that I did hear the tide playing between the rocks and singing over sands. Wooded glens I saw there, waterfalls and mountains. I pulled for very life; but, for as near as I was, no nearer in my curragh did I get. Even as I looked the land went down, sudden as it did come up. My sorrow, there was nothing left but the wide, wide ocean. No gift I had to throw upon that shore to fix it." Without the gift to throw on Tir nan Ogue, the saying is, no man can stay it. . . . A few years since on this wild lonely road at Crohan's foot a cry arose one Sunday from those who came from mass: "See that land!" said one; and not far out these people swore to me that in the ocean they had seen an island rise with mountains, woods and glens, and that as they stood astonied, it vanished down into the sea.

To the Watchers or Shepherd People I have alluded, whom the Gnostics called "Weavers of the Vesture of Light," also "Heralds or Treasurers of Light." The Quartemary relates to the Kingdom of Law. The fundamental Law is in the mystery of the Quartemary, Justice, Prudence, Fortitude, and Love. The Quartemary is under the dominion of the Rulers of the Aeons, according to the Gnostics, i.e. the Lower Aspect of the seven planets. Humanity is evoluting down here in that Quartemary. The Triad relates to the Kingdom of Heaven or Spirit, the number of the Divinity, Spirit, Soul, and Body. It is a magnificent mysticism, the mysticism of the mountains and their rulers as it is revealed to the seer, however dimly.

Every mountain is under a Ray of the Watchers, the Ray of the Seraphs comes straight from the Watchers in the Upper Triad, that is to say, the third World or Zone, into which Manaan has merged. Great influences or emanations are permeating the divine reality of our mountains, for the servants of the hills are a mighty race. The power of Great Cuchullin is in air, in rocks, and stones. But many names given us are probably blinds to us. It may be that to the greatest seers is manifested but the fringe or outer aspect of the mystery in which those spirit-rulers dwell.

In New Grange, The Brughna or Temple of the Boyne, Aengus Oge, the young God of Beauty, Master of Love makes his dwelling; he is seen pervading the whole of Ireland; "Angus of the Birds," he is called by the people, because to those who see him floating over sea and land, round his head appear the immortal rainbow-colored birds who are the children of his breath. Slieve Namon, County Tipperary, is the Mountain of Sound. Messages are breathed there to psychic ears in supreme orchestral harmonies.

Dana herself is seen—The Ageless Mother of the ancient Celtic gods who pervades the kingdom of sky, who sways on earth and sea the world of energies—the world of yet unknown vibrations— floating irradiant in aureoles of transcendental light, —filling the Nature world with mystery, stepping the Isle of Destiny; brown Mother-Earth, the Great Enchantress of my feet, when wandering up the shifting ways; invoked by the poet thus— "Dumb Mother struggling through the years to tell Her secret out through helpless eyes"; she whose presence in Ireland inspired the lovely lines in the soul of one who sees . .

" *I can enchant the trees and rocks, and fill*

The dumb brown lips of earth with mystery.

Make them reveal or hide the god. I breathe

A deeper pity than all love, myself

Mother of all, but without hands to heal:

Too vast and vague, they know me not. But yet.

I am the heartbreak over fallen things,

The sudden gentleness that stays the blow,

And I am in the kiss that foemen give,

Pausing in battle, and in the tears that fall

Over the vanquished foe, and in the highest

Among the Danaan gods, I am the last

Council of mercy in their hearts, where they

Mete justice from a thousand starry thrones."